DANTE'S
DIVINE COMEDY

THE LANDMARK LIBRARY

Chapters in the History of Civilization

The Landmark Library is a record of the achievements of humankind from the late Stone Age to the present day. Each volume in the series is devoted to a crucial theme in the history of civilization, and offers a concise and authoritative text accompanied by a generous complement of images. Contributing authors to the Landmark Library are chosen for their ability to combine scholarship with a flair for communicating their specialist knowledge to a wider, non-specialist readership.

DANTE'S DIVINE COMEDY

A Journey Without End

IAN THOMSON

HEAD of ZEUS

An Apollo Book

For the silver screen flimmers.
Poca favilla gran fiamma seconda

This Apollo book was first published in the UK in 2018 by Head of Zeus Ltd.
This paperback edition first published in the UK in 2021 by Head of Zeus Ltd.

1 3 5 7 9 10 8 6 4 2

A CIP catalogue record for this book is available from the British Library.

ISBN (PB) 9781789548778
ISBN (E) 9781786690791

Designed by Isambard Thomas
Printed in Spain by Graficas Estella

Head of Zeus Ltd
First Floor East
5–8 Hardwick Street
London EC1R 4RG

WWW.HEADOFZEUS.COM

PREVIOUS PAGES
Domenico di Michelino's 1456 *La commedia illumina Firenze* (The Comedy Illuminates Florence), located on the west wall of the Duomo in Florence.

IMAGE CREDITS
Cover Dante in his Study © Tom Phillips. All Rights Reserved, DACS 2018. pp. 4–5 Getty/DEA/G. Dagli Orti; p. 18 Splash News/Alamy; p. 20 © Tate, London 2018; p. 22 Getty/Historical Picture Archive; pp. 24–5, 28–9 Fox/Kobal/REX/Shutterstock; p. 31 Everett Collection Inc./Alamy; p. 34 © Alma Books; pp. 38–9 Peter Barritt/Alamy; p. 49 Shutterstock; pp. 66–7 Harvard Art Museums/Fogg Museum, Bequest of Grenville L. Winthrop; p. 72 Getty/DEA/Veneranda Biblioteca Ambrosiana; p. 87 Leemage/Contributor; p. 103 De Agostini Picture Library/G. Nimatallah/Bridgeman; pp. 109–10 Getty, Franco Origlia; p. 126 Getty/Ulf Andersen; p. 137 Granger/Bridgeman; p. 139 © British Library Board/Bridgeman; p. 148 Granger/Alamy; p. 158 Mondadori Portfolio/Bridgeman; pp. 168–9 Fratelli Alinari/Getty; pp. 188–9 Peter Horree/Alamy; p. 211 Getty/David Lees; p. 226 AP/Topfoto.co.uk; p. 231 akg-images/Mondadori Portfolio/Electa/Saporetti; p. 235 © Robert Rauschenberg Foundation/DACS, London/VAGA, NY 2018, Canto IV: Limbo, Circle One, The Virtuous Pagans from Thirty-Four Illustrations for Dante's *Inferno* (1959–60), MoMA; p. 236 Wellcome Images/Getty; p. 242–3 Getty/Heritage Images; p. 245 Cornell University Library; pp. 246¬–7 akg-images/André Held; pp. 256–7 Getty/Heritage Images; p. 263 Galleria degli Uffizi, Florence/Bridgeman; pp. 50–1, 54–5, 80, 98, 128, 147, 154–5, 176–7, 200–1, 206–7, 264, 288–9 Public Domain/Wikimedia Commons.

'To understand Dante it is not, of course, necessary to believe what he believed, but it is, I think, necessary to understand what he believed.'

DOROTHY L. SAYERS

'Before you know it, you're in the noisome regions of the night'

LOUIS-FERDINAND CÉLINE,
JOURNEY TO THE END OF THE NIGHT

VERY LATE NEWS
Dante in Ferno Shock

After a turbulent 12 months
of unprecedented upheaval,
the 14th Century poet and creator
of the Divine Comedy, Dante
Alighieri, admitted today that he'll
be glad to see the back of this year,
saying 'Phew, I've been trapped
in this circle of hell for so long,
I can't wait to get out of it. It's such
a relief to know that the fourth circle
of hell is over!'

PRIVATE EYE,
23 DECEMBER–12 JANUARY 2017

Note to the reader

Except for *The Divine Comedy,* I use the Italian or Latin titles for Dante's work, though some titles remain disputed. For example, rather than the Italian *Vita nuova,* Dante's title is now thought to have been the Latin *Vita nova,* after the line in the opening paragraph: '*Incipit vita nova*'. (I have kept to the customary *Vita nuova.*) All translations of quotations are my own, unless otherwise indicated.

Introduction:
A Divine Journey
to Hell and Back

'*The Divine Comedy* is a book that
everyone ought to read.'

JORGE LUIS BORGES

As every Italian schoolchild knows, *The Divine Comedy* opens in a supernatural dark wood just before sunrise on Good Friday, 1300. Dante Alighieri, a figure in his own work, has lost his way in middle age and is alone and frightened in the darkness. At the request of a woman called Beatrice, the ghost of the Roman poet Virgil is about to show him Hell.

> Midway in the journey of our life
> I found myself in a dark wood,
> for the right path was lost

Begun in the first decade of the fourteenth century, Dante's poem is, for many, the greatest single work of Western literature. It gathers together an extraordinary range of literary styles: lyric, satiric, biblical and invective. The poem's bold intermixture of realities, from the sublime to the vile, is part of what makes it so modern. Much of *The Divine Comedy* is composed in the Italian vernacular which Dante regarded as the true and richly storied expression of the Italian people. Dante said he owed his 'life' to this vernacular, meaning that it was his parents' native tongue. Even when *The Divine Comedy* aspires to grandiloquence with mannered and evocative Latinisms, the language stays close to everyday usage. Dante's unfinished treatise, *De vulgari eloquentia* (On Eloquence in the Vernacular), written some time between 1302 and 1305, is an impassioned plea for linguistic unity in a peninsula divided by over thirty dialects. Dante would not have been referred to as 'Italian' in his day because Italy as a nation-state did not exist until unification in 1861. Only then could Dante become Italy's *Sommo Poeta*, Supreme Poet.

The Divine Comedy, with its dramatic chiaroscuro of fuming mists and frozen shallows, is 'awful' in that archaic sense of the word (still valid in the Italian *terribile*) meaning to inspire awe. It is divided into three books or canticles of equal length: *Inferno, Purgatorio, Paradiso*. Each canticle is made up of thirty-three rhymed sections called cantos, with an additional introductory canto for the *Inferno*. One hundred cantos in all. The poem is called a 'comedy' in the medieval-Aristotelian sense that it leads from misery to a state of happiness. Dante's salvation is 'comic' in that it culminates in joy.

In the course of his poem Dante is seen to fathom the nine concentric circles of hell, before his ascent to the summit of Mount Purgatory takes him to the revelation of God in Paradise. The theme of despair ascending through hope towards salvation is Catholic. In medieval Catholic orthodoxy, Purgatory was an in-between state where imperfect souls were cleansed by fire in preparation for their entry into heaven. Dante's journey from the supernatural 'dark wood' to heaven by way of Purgatory lasts just one week, in a poem that took over twelve years to complete. Having journeyed through a strange tragic land populated by the guilty dead, Dante is re-conducted to a world of light. His intention all along had been to write *in pro del mondo che mal vive* ('for the benefit of the world which lives badly').

Given our distance from medieval theology, the poet's three-part journey into the afterlife may at times be hard for us to understand. Attitudes to medieval worship changed in Northern Europe after the Protestant Reformation. The architect of King Henry VIII's religious reforms in England, the statesman-lawyer Thomas Cromwell, wanted to uproot Catholic belief in hellfire, Purgatory, Marian intercession and other papistical 'abominations'. *The Divine Comedy*, with its animus against papal and clerical corruptions, was used as Protestant justification for why the pope should no longer remain head of the church in Tudor England. Dante portrayed a pope during his lifetime, Boniface VIII, as a ravaging wolf who gulled congregations into false absolution. This Antichrist pope had turned the Holy See into a *cloaca del sangue e de la puzza* (a 'sewer of blood and stench').

During the Reformation, Dante's antipapal status was confirmed by Protestant polemic which vilified Rome as an impious, jewel-eyed harlot. One of the most influential religious books in England at this time, Foxe's 1563 *Book of Martyrs*, applauded Dante as 'an Italian writer against the pope'. Of course *The Divine Comedy* is not an anti-Catholic work at all. Tommaso Campanella, the Dominican philosopher who was charged with heresy in 1599, admired the poem because it 'teaches in a popular fashion how to live according to Catholic belief'. *The Divine Comedy* belongs to a pre-Reformation world where any pity shown to the damned was seen as an offence against divine justice. Always, Dante is careful to distinguish between Catholicism and a corrupt papacy.

The *Inferno* contains scenes of extravagant cruelty. The reader looks on aghast as money-brokers, corrupted popes, as well as fate-smitten figures from Classical Greek and Roman mythology, address Dante directly from the flames of damnation. The sounds and signs of physical pain are everywhere present. Many of Dante's damned creatures curse God, others confront Him in anger; none complains that his or her punishment is unjust. The dominant theme of the *Inferno* is justice, rigidly applied. The absence of forgiveness in a manifestly Christian poem may be striking, but the medieval world insisted on the eternity of punishment; in some ways the *Inferno* is a giant judicial machine in which God's justice is vindicated before men.

Unsurprisingly the *Inferno* remains the most popular of the poem's three canticles. While the hell-pit torments were not all of Dante's devising (they were displayed in Florentine church frescoes and recited in ghoulish rhyme by pantomime street devils), they remain the most original and audacious treatment of the afterlife in Western literature. The *Inferno* has inspired a number of sulphurous literary works, from James Thomson's nineteenth-century epic poem *The City of Dreadful Night* to

Malcolm Lowry's novel *Under the Volcano,* whose horny-browed devils and other Mexican grotesqueries surely emerged from the charnel house of Dante's imagination. Dantescan, too, are the hell sermons in James Joyce's *Portrait of the Artist as a Young Man*, where a Catholic priest yells 'Hell!' five times in an attempt to still fear into his audience. Victorian-era illustrations to the *Inferno* by Gustave Doré were no less disconcerting; the damned are shown wedged 'arsy-versy' against each other in snake pits, 'watering their bottoms with their tears', as Samuel Beckett put it in his 1976 Dantescan prose work *All Strange Away.*

Comparatively few people are moved to read *Purgatorio* or *Paradiso,* though Dante's poetry is at its most entrancing in those two canticles. The truth was, Dante did not want his readers to dally over-long in Hell as *The Divine Comedy* would be incomplete unless they apprehended the whole. The vision of Satan at the end of the *Inferno* as a three-faced, shaggy-haired monstrosity is fittingly ridiculous and anti-climactic. The *Inferno* is where the *damned* stay immobilized by their own bad choices, and for that reason alone it should not be where the entire poem ends. To most twenty-first-century readers the *Inferno* nevertheless *is* Dante, with *Purgatorio* and *Paradiso* seen as a distinct falling off from that first great canticle. Victor Hugo went so far as to claim that the human eye was not made to look at the light of Dante's Paradise: 'when the poem becomes happy, it becomes boring.' For Hugo, as for many readers after him, the *Inferno* was the really 'interesting' canticle, where a recognizable human drama of guilty love, transgression and punishment is depicted. The siren call of damnation calls to us in a way that Dante's emotional rescue and atonement clearly do not. (In the US television series *Mad Men* the charmingly mendacious adulterer Don Draper is thus seen reading a copy of the *Inferno* while on a beach in Miami.)

Dante's vision of self-knowledge and deliverance soars above all poetry of the late Middle Ages. There is such grave religious

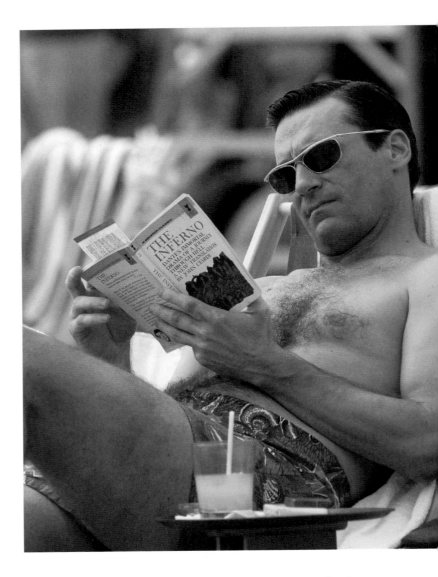

Don Draper, during *Mad Men*'s sixth season, on a Hawaiian beach reading a paperback of John Ciardi's 1954 translation of the *Inferno*.

intent in *The Divine Comedy* – the unflinching look at sin, the stony steps towards salvation – that some have misconstrued it as a dreary work of medieval theism. Voltaire made no mention of Dante in his 1727 *Essay on Epic Poetry* as he viewed Dante as a poet of the darkest superstitions of an unenlightened age, and thus a product of the bigotry and fanaticism which had atrophied *ancien régime* Europe. An image has persisted ever since of Dante as a sour, ascetic poet driven by a demon of retribution. Friedrich Nietzsche was not alone in dismissing him as a 'hyena' making verses among the tombs. Into his poem Dante certainly brought personal animosities and rancour; but also a generous and patriotic indignation, tender memories of friends, masters and companions. Lord Byron's 'grim Dante' did more than put his friends in Paradise and foes in Hell; in *Purgatorio* and *Paradiso* alike we find Dante homely, humorous and tender and, in the presence of Beatrice, exultant. The gentleness of Dante goes 'beyond all gentleness', Byron reckoned. For these and other reasons *The Divine Comedy* remains a pillar of the European literary canon.

*

Central to the poem is Dante's meditation on the mystery of love. Scholars have long puzzled over the nature of the poet's love for Beatrice dei Portinari. Did Beatrice even exist? Little is known of her, though she was the flame of Dante's life and the subject of his great first book, *La vita nuova* (*The New Life*), a spiritual memoir held together by a sequence of beautiful poems. Purportedly Beatrice died in her birthplace of Florence in 1290 at the age of only twenty-four. Dante was left bereft. Throughout *The Divine Comedy* she is divine grace and the embodiment therefore of a revealed Catholic ideology. While Beatrice does not appear until midway through the poem (as a veiled woman in robes the colour of 'living flame'), right from the start she is identified as the voice which addresses Virgil from Heaven. Dante's salvation is already complete when Virgil finally surrenders his role as guide to Beatrice. From Beatrice, now unveiled, Dante then hears one of the most beautifully spare declarations of love in all literature: '*Guardami ben: io son, io son, Beatrice*' ('Look on me well: I am, I truly am, Beatrice').

The Divine Comedy was the first literary work to elevate a woman as guide to an other-worldly realm. In the third and final canticle, *Paradiso*, Beatrice is a sort of stellar enchantment of the universe, who leads Dante to 'the Love which moves the sun and other stars' ('*l'amor che move il sole e l'altre stelle*'): that is, to God. Her shining figure was ahead of its time. Beatrice's ringing attack in canto 29 of *Paradiso* on preachers who pervert the gospel must have disconcerted some clerical audiences: St Paul had forbidden woman to teach and 'exercise authority over man'.

The story of Dante's love for Beatrice occurs with dizzying frequency in Victorian poems, paintings and, of course, sermons. Like the Lady of Shallot or Florence Nightingale, for the Pre-Raphaelites Beatrice was a chivalrous ideal of perfection and sanctifying love. Love prompts her to intercede and call on Virgil to rescue Dante in the dangerous wildwoods of the poem's first canto ('*amor mi mosse*', she tells Dante, 'love moved me'). Appropriately her name means 'she who makes blessed'. Dante's love for Beatrice is the greatest of all love affairs and certainly the most sustained and unusual narrative of love in any book. The twentieth-century critic and novelist Charles Williams explored the nature of that love in his tour de force of literary imagination, *The Figure of Beatrice*; hugely admired on its publication in 1944, Williams' is a hard-to-define and occasionally blurry work of scholarship with an undertow of Anglo-Catholic mysticism. By the late 1940s, however, Williams had put his name to an entire field of Beatrice studies. (His supernatural thrillers were much admired by T. S. Eliot.)

Beata Beatrix (Blessed Beatrice) by the Pre-Raphaelite painter and poet Dante Gabriel Rossetti. Beatrice is modelled on Rossetti's deceased wife Elizabeth Siddal, who died in 1862 of a drug overdose.

Today the *Inferno* is present in a surprising array of popular books and media, from the Lemony Snicket series for children to Japanese anime films and the *Doom* video games, with their murky lore referring to 'nine circles' and the 'Doomslayer' (or 'Hell Walker'). Dan Brown's *Inferno,* the fastest-selling novel of 2013, was a bibliographic thriller whose sleuth-hero Robert Langdon is lost in a labyrinth of Dantean symbols and codes. Of course, where Dante's '*Inferno*' is awful in the sense of inspiring awe, it could be argued that Brown's is merely awful. ('A powerfully built woman effortlessly unstraddled her BMW motorcycle...')

*

Dante began to write *The Divine Comedy* in around 1308, six years after his expulsion from Florence in 1302 on corruption, embezzlement and other charges. The charges were mostly false yet Dante never again set foot in his native Florence. He completed *The Divine Comedy* in Ravenna, where he died in 1321, and lies buried. Exile allowed him to work on his private vision of Hell, and exact a pitiless revenge on the humbugs (as he saw them) who had ruined Florence through their double standards and unrighteous gains. Prelates, politicians and other fallen people are boiled alive in tar, trapped in ice, or submerged in stinking hell-pits. The further we climb down with Dante through Hell, the more the poet's seemingly vengeful nature prevails. Prostitutes ('that tart Cleopatra'), corrupted bankers, money-lenders, love-cheats, negligent and corrupt rulers; the unabsolved, the indolent and the excommunicate: all are consigned to flame, besmeared in shite or submerged in pitch. Dante's portrayal of the living dead anticipates the Romantic creation of horror. The Palace of Subterranean Fire in William Beckford's 1782 chain-rattling Gothic novel, *Vathek*, is the first atrocious Hell in modern times

The Pre-Raphaelite painter John Everett Millais dressed as Dante in a glass-plate negative from 1862. To the Pre-Raphaelites Dante was a literary hero.

overleaf Spencer Tracy gazing at a bust of Dante in the 1935 film *Dante's Inferno.* A character in the film says: 'The message he gave to the world in his story of the *Inferno* burns as brightly today as when he wrote it.'

influenced by Dante. Romantic horror also informs the 1935 movie melodrama *Dante's Inferno,* starring Spencer Tracy as a ruthlessly ambitious circus manager who inherits a fairground attraction called 'Dante's Inferno'. The film offers a ten-minute reconstruction of a Dantescan underworld complete with howling naked shades, writhing serpents, dismal trenches and, above it all, Satan's baleful reign. Modelled on Doré's Victorian-era illustrations, there is nothing quite like it in 20th Century Fox history.

*

Dante speaks to us today not because we fear damnation or are moved by the beauty of the Christian revelation, but because he wrote the story of an ordinary man – an Everyman – who sets out hopefully in this life in search of renewal. The poem is a pilgrimage of sorts – an act of turning to a better life. Dante's moral progress in *The Divine Comedy* was part of a medieval reality. An actual pilgrimage to Jerusalem, Rome, Compostela or (as Chaucer reminds us) Canterbury could lessen not only one's own afterlife penance but also that of deceased loved ones who were already in Purgatory's refining fires.

No complete English translation of *La divina commedia* existed by the time John Bunyan came to write *The Pilgrim's Progress* in 1660s England, yet the journeying metaphor of Everyman informs Bunyan's Christian allegory, as it did Dante's. Throughout his own poem, Dante is a '*persona umile e peregrina*' ('a humble person on a journey'), who moves from a state of penitential barrenness to one of grace. Joseph Luzzi, the distinguished American professor of Dante studies, was hurled into an inferno in 2007 when his wife Katherine was killed in a car accident in New York state. Luzzi's memoir, *In a Dark Wood,* tells how their baby daughter was delivered by caesarean just forty-five minutes before the doctors pronounced Katherine dead. Alone and widowed in Dante's 'dark wood', Luzzi was able eventually to find a design for his shattered life in *The Divine Comedy*.

*

In order to reach a wide audience Dante chose to write *The Divine Comedy* not in Latin, but in the easily understood vernacular of his own Florence. No work of the late medieval or early Renaissance period had rejected literary and church Latin so absolutely. Latin was spoken by the educated elite of Western and Central Europe; all serious thinking and even some speaking was conducted in Latin. Church Latin was thought to be particularly suited to expounding the unchanging truths which formed the preserve of man's 'higher reason'. Compared to the grace and suppleness of Tuscan, however, Latin was abstract, static and cumbersome. Tuscan was a language close to the soil and the marketplace; it was a spoken rather than a written language and not without its vulgarisms and pungent invective. Appropriately, the most common word in *The Divine Comedy* is *terra* (earth): Dante wrote in a language that was spoken in the streets of his own town and in the surrounding countryside. The poem's first readers were Florentine wool merchants, tavern-keepers and craftsmen who had little or no knowledge of Latin, as well as courtiers, princes and prelates.

Dante's decision to write in his native Tuscan idiom was a moment of extraordinary significance in the history of Western civilization. His rejection of Latin preceded Chaucer's by eighty years, and ensured that Tuscan would become Italy's literary language and, eventually, its national language. If Dante is revered as the patriarch of modern letters it is chiefly because of his 'invention' of Italian. At the beginning of the fourteenth century

overleaf
Hell Scene from the 1935 Hollywood film *Dante's Inferno*, directed by the post-Impressionist painter Harry Lachman. Ken Russell intercut footage from this film in his 1980 sci-fi thriller *Altered States*.

the Italian peninsula was made up of a number of city-states, each with its own vernacular based on 'vulgar' Latin of which the *dialetto toscano* (Tuscan dialect) was but one. In *The Divine Comedy* the term for Italians is *latini*, and for Italy, *terra Latina*. Italian – that is, a common language used across the peninsula – had yet to be born. It is curious to reflect that Italian today might be a quite different language had Dante come from Milan, say, or Palermo.

To date, over 800 pre-Gutenberg press manuscripts of *The Divine Comedy* are known to exist, yet no original manuscript of the poem has survived in Dante's own hand. The first copies were made by scribes; many of these are sumptuously illustrated calligraphic masterworks, but others are marred by erasures, scrapings, jumbled foliations and scribal errors. Humidity and rats have also done their damage (parchment is protein and edible). The first printed edition of *The Divine Comedy,* issued in Umbria in 1472 by the German cleric-printer Johannes Neumeister, had attractively clear Gothic letters; but it contained errors. The smallest-sized Dante in the world, '*Il Dantino*' ('The Little Dante'), was no less corrupted by printer's errors. Published in Milan in 1878, the book measured 5.7 by 4.4 centimetres and was supposed to fit into a waistcoat pocket. Impossible to read without a powerful magnifying glass, '*Il Dantino*' was exhibited at the 1878 Universal Exposition in Paris as an 'outstanding example of typographical achievement'.

The standard critical edition of *The Divine Comedy* – the one used today by academics and by interested lay readers alike – was edited by Giorgio Petrocchi between 1966 and 1967. Many scholars doubt whether it is feasible to establish a critical edition of Dante's poem; yet the biblio-sleuth in Petrocchi set out to divine the hidden 'true' Dante from among the thirty-odd early Florentine manuscripts under his scrutiny. The manuscripts all predated the editorial endeavours of the Florentine writer

The Italian writer-chemist Primo Levi in 1940, three years before he was arrested by Italian fascists and deported to Auschwitz. Dante's influence pervades Levi's Auschwitz camp memoir, *If This is a Man*.

DANTE'S DIVINE COMEDY

Giovanni Boccaccio (author of the *Decameron* and Dante's first biographer), who meddled with and contaminated the original after copying it out at least three times between the mid-1350s and 1373. It was Boccaccio, incidentally, who first applied the epithet 'Divine' to a poem which Dante had simply called the *Comedy* (though some scholars insist that '*Divina*' was not added until 1555 – by a Venetian printer).

Eighty per cent of Petrocchi's four-volume 'national' edition (known as 'The *Comedy* According to the Ancient Vulgate') is today immediately comprehensible to Italian ears, while Chaucer's Middle English is liable to defeat most Britons. Dante's poem is studied in Italy at school, praised by the Holy See, printed on T-shirts, applauded in the Senate and quoted on the streets. As a teenager in his native Turin the Italian writer-chemist Primo Levi took part in outdoor 'Dante tournaments' where boys flaunted their knowledge of *The Divine Comedy*, with a competitor reciting a canto and his rival scoring a point if he knew its continuation. In his 1947 concentration camp memoir *If This is a Man*, Levi relates how he struggled at Auschwitz to remember lines from Dante's poem. He and a French prisoner, Jean Samuel, had set out to collect the soup ration one day in 1944, when canto 26 of the *Inferno* came back to memory. The classical Greek hero Ulysses is addressing his ship's crew as they embark on their final voyage before the sea sucks them under:

> '*Think on why you were created:*
> not to live as brutes merely,
> but to follow after knowledge and good.'

In the hell of Auschwitz, *anus mundi*, Ulysses' commendation to know and understand radiates a sublime dignity. Dante's vision of human knowledge and endeavour in canto 26 will lie at the heart of the Italian Renaissance: *The Divine Comedy* might be seen as the first great step from Gothic darkness into the light of the pre-Renaissance. So Primo Levi and Jean Samuel are not *Untermenschen* (sub-humans) as the Nazi race scientists had declared Jews to be; they were made 'men' in order to pursue knowledge. Some have asked whether Levi really had recalled lines by Dante at Auschwitz: the counterpoint of poetic beauty in such a vile place might suggest the artifice of afterthought. Yet Levi was among the last generation of Italians to be taught largely by rote; every one of those words from the Ulysses canto (and more) was committed to his memory.

*

The *Inferno* is the most widely translated book after the Bible, with at least fifty English-language versions in the twentieth century alone. Translations tell us much about changing attitudes to Dante. The Victorians were prone to reduce the poet's crystalline cantos to a sort of pious fustian, full of righteous morality. There was a message in *The Divine Comedy* which solemn-minded Christians such as John Ruskin saw as their duty to convey: the wages of sin shall be known in Purgatory. Yet, awkwardly for the Victorians, the poem is decidedly ribald in parts. When William Burroughs's hallucinated novel *Naked Lunch* was prosecuted for obscenity in Boston in 1965 (the uproarious 'talking asshole' chapter), Dante was cited in the novel's defence. Like an outdoor lavatory Dante, quite as much as Burroughs, can still take some getting used to.

The poet's influence on contemporary American and British writing is alive and vital. The poet Craig Raine's 2012 novel, *The Divine Comedy,* set in post-communist Poland, looks unflinchingly at the mortifications and functions of the human body: the embarrassment of flatulence, the wayward thrills (as one character sees it) of flagellation. Dantescan punishments are meted out to adulterers, who die in car crashes or develop cancer.

Cover of the 1964 UK edition of William Burroughs's controversial novel *The Naked Lunch*. Dante was cited in the novel's defence at the 1965 Boston obscenity trial.

'Dante knew what he was talking about', the Catholic convert Robert Lowell wrote to Ezra Pound in 1954, meaning perhaps that Dante understood the cost of sin. (A more recent sinner, the British author Jeffrey Archer, chose to subtitle the three volumes of his prison memoir *Hell*, *Purgatory* and *Heaven*.)

James Joyce, for his part, proclaimed an undying admiration for *The Divine Comedy*: 'I love my Dante as much as the Bible,' he said, adding: 'He is my spiritual food, the rest is ballast.' All life is contained in the poem, for Dante's was an all-encompassing imagination, that interwove classical philosophy with Catholic doctrine and contemporary politics. Honoré de Balzac in his *Comédie humaine* (1842–53) consciously sought to emulate the great human variety and detail of Dante's poem. Another *dantista*, the Russian poet Osip Mandelstam, never left his Moscow flat during the Stalin oppressions without a paperback Dante in the event of his arrest. The darker woes to be found in Dante – the long nights of darkness and dismay – were familiar to Mandelstam as they were to Oscar Wilde and other writers unjustly persecuted and imprisoned.

In 1882, in a foretaste of his own arrest fourteen years later, Wilde was invited to inspect a Nebraskan penitentiary during his lecture tour of America. To his surprise he found a copy there of *The Divine Comedy* illustrated by Doré. 'Oh dear, who would have thought of finding Dante here?' Perhaps the governors hoped to edify the inmates. To Helena Sickert, sister of the painter Walter Sickert, Wilde wrote: 'Strange and beautiful it seemed to me that the sorrow of a single Florentine in exile should, hundreds of years afterwards, lighten the sorrow of some common prisoner in a modern gaol.' Wilde would remember to ask for a copy of Dante when in prison himself on a charge of 'gross indecency', even though *The Divine Comedy* accounts homosexuality an offence almost too grievous to be atoned for.

Of all the monotheist religions, Islam is the richest in legends of the afterlife. The Koran abounds in detailed descriptions of the abodes and lives of blessed and wicked souls. Dante may have had these in mind when he came to write parts of *The Divine Comedy*, brocaded as they are with Arabo-Islamic words such as 'assassin', 'alchemy', 'zenith' and 'alcohol'. However, the poem subjects the Prophet Muhammad to a grotesque punishment, his body split from end to end so that his entrails dangle out amid excrement.

Is the punishment really (as one historian insists) a 'peculiarly disgusting' target of Western Orientalism? In the *Inferno* human bodies are frequently twisted, torn, pricked and gnawed at by devils and harpies. Whether they are Muslim or Christian (most of them are Christian), it is worth noting that Dante subjects them all to the same merciless sword. Obviously, Dante cannot be judged by the standards of today, yet his portrayal of the Prophet remains offensive to a strain of Islamic culture. In recent times, Muslim responses to *The Divine Comedy* have ranged from the considered and scholarly to the downright murderous. The Persian translation of *The Divine Comedy* by the Tehran poet Farideh Mahdavi-Damghani, published in 1999, expurgates all mention of the Prophet, as does (presumably on grounds of political correctness) the 2012 comic strip version of *Dante's Inferno* by Hunt Emerson and Kevin Jackson. 'Because of our profound respect for the noble religion of Islam and its followers', writes Jackson, 'we have omitted this section.' The gulf between the Christian West and the Islamic East – the rising rhetoric of a perceived 'clash of civilizations' – is of course aggravated by perceived slights to the Prophet. In 1938, a reprint in Hindustani of H. G. Wells's *Short History of the World* provoked the first recorded Muslim book burning in Britain: Wells, like Dante before him, had described the Prophet as a 'man...of considerable vanity, greed, cunning and self-deception'; by symbolically burning the book, East London's Muslim community hoped that the offence done to Islam might be assuaged. In 2002 there was a plot to blow up Bologna Cathedral on account of its fifteenth-century fresco depicting Muhammad tormented by devils in a Last Judgment scene by Giovanni da Modena, inspired by Dante. Why exactly Dante chose to doom Muhammad to Hell is a question that this book will seek to clarify.

*

A great deal of recent scholarship has been devoted to Dante's attitude to women and gender, but very little to Dante and music. Dante had evidently studied music, and was accustomed to hearing it well performed. Many composers have wondered if *The Divine Comedy* might translate into music. Dante's famous inscription over the gates of Hell – 'ABANDON ALL HOPE, YOU WHO ENTER HERE' – is bruited out onomatopoeically at the beginning of Franz Liszt's *Dante Symphony* of 1856. In a peculiar sense, Liszt's tone poem (it is not really a symphony), with its grand chord laments and tense interludes of silence, suggests a horror-film soundtrack. Only one Italian composer planned a work on all three parts of *The Divine Comedy*. This was the Tuscan-born Giacomo Puccini, whose opera *Gianni Schicchi* is based on a character from Dante's *Inferno*. In Italy on the eve of the Great War, Dante inevitably took on new meanings and a national significance. Mussolini's favourite author, the Italian poet-aviator Gabriele d'Annunzio, provided the libretto for a 1914 Dante opera by Riccardo Zandonai, *Francesca da Rimini*. Zandonai's is a dainty piece of music redolent of pink lampshades and rustling frou-frous; it suits the libretto's air of decadent languor. Today d'Annunzio is regarded more or less as a dilettante of sensation.

overleaf   *Lucifer Eating Sinners* by Giovanni da Modena, 1410. On Lucifer's right is Muhammad, a naked elderly man, tied to a rock while a demon tortures him. The caption 'Machomet' (an uncommon spelling of Muhammad) is visible on the rock.

His poem '*Due Beatrici*' ('Two Beatrices') exalts Dante's Florentine muse as a dewy-eyed damsel, tender as a marshmallow.

The 1960s, happily, saw a number of distinguished avant-garde interpretations of Dante-in-music. Luciano Berio, the 'Godfather of Italian composition', was a magpie-like pasticheur who stole from a variety of sources ranging from Sicilian folksong to the Beatles. In February 1966 he gave a lecture on Dante at the Italian Cultural Institute in London. The forty-one-year-old Italian composer was by then a big enough name to attract the attention of Paul McCartney, who admired Berio's 1963–5 homage to Dante, *Laborintus II*, where skewed jazz rhythms and words by the Genoese poet Eduardo Sanguinetti represent the grafters and money-brokers of Hell. (The piece was written to commemorate the 700th year of Dante's birth.) McCartney turned up at Berio's lecture in his Aston Martin, and in the interval chatted briefly with the composer about *The Divine Comedy* while newspaper photographers intruded noisily. The affront to Berio caused by an uncomprehending British press upset McCartney more than any intrusions on his own life. 'Why don't *you* create something?' the Beatle yelled at the jostling cameramen. (The *Daily Mail*'s sarcastic headline next morning was 'THIS IS WHAT A BEATLE DOES IN THE EVENING'.) In more recent times, the maverick front-man of the British post-punk band The Fall, the late Mark E. Smith, declared that 'writing about Prestwich is just as valid as Dante writing about his inferno'. As far as Smith was concerned, the *Inferno* was no curio from a superseded medieval world. Out of Prestwich (the Manchester town where The Fall was founded in 1976) he created an image of a dead-dull Dantean nowhere. A new kind of pop vernacular.

Dante's continued relevance for the secular west was advanced by Robert Rauschenberg, the self-anointed 'bad boy' of contemporary American art, who between 1958 and 1960 executed a series of works on the theme of damnation inspired by John Ciardi's bestselling English translation of the *Inferno*. Rauschenberg's Dante cycle – one delicate translucency for each of the canticle's thirty-four cantos – was admired by Samuel Beckett, for one, who tried (but failed) to see it on display in Berlin in 1965. Beckett kept a copy of *The Divine Comedy* by his bedside as he lay dying in a Paris hospice in 1989. Oxygen canisters stood nearby for his emphysema but, immersed in Dante, he appeared to be 'having fun', remembered the poet Derek Mahon (who visited him a month before he died at the age of eighty-three). The ninth monologue of Beckett's 1954 *Texts for Nothing* offers a literal translation of the four concluding words of the *Inferno:* 'and see the stars again' ('*a riveder le stelle*'). They are spoken by a tramp-like waif as he contemplates death.

> There's a way out there, there's a way out somewhere, the rest would come, the other words, sooner or later, and the power to get there, and the way to get there, and pass out, and see the beauties of the skies, and see the stars again.

On his resurgence from the death-like impasse of Hell Dante Alighieri too will 'see the stars again'.

Ian Thomson,
London, June 2018

Guelfs v. Ghibellines

Dante Alighieri was born in Florence in 1265 in the San Pier Maggiore district situated between the present-day Duomo and Piazza della Signoria. San Pier Maggiore was a respectable *sestiere* or administrative division of the Tuscan city inhabited by aristocrats, as well as by artisans, merchants and others less socially elevated. (The Casa di Dante shown to tourists in Florence was built largely in the early twentieth century.) The Florence in which Dante lived was one of the richest and most populous cities in Europe – far larger than London. Dante's father, Alighiero di Bellincione (born in about 1220), was a notary who belonged to the middle-ranking Florentine merchant aristocracy. The family name of Alighieri is thought to mean 'wing-bearer' from the Latin *aliger*, winged. The poet's given name, Durante, has no Christian significance but this was quite usual in thirteenth-century Florence, when only a quarter of Italian children were named after the Catholic saints. Durante, meaning 'he who endures' or 'who resists', was later shortened to Dante.

Dante's father exercised no political power, but, as one of the Florentine *eminenti*, he owned two good-sized farms outside the city: one near Fiesole; the other near Pontassieve. He could afford to educate his children. As a canny steward he let out his estates to tenant farmers. Outwardly a man of probity, his main business was nevertheless hostile to Christian morality. Alighieri was involved in money-lending; it was reckoned to be wrong to make money speculatively, that is from the future, because the future belonged to God alone. The business was later condemned by Dante as 'usury' (though without the usual, anti-Judaic connotations). Consigned to the seventh circle of Hell alongside blasphemers and sodomites, usurers are made to stare at the sacks of lucre hanging heavy round their necks. The sacks, emblazoned with fancy coats of arms, would have held the equivalent of today's venture capitalist bonus payments. The reader might be forgiven for thinking that 'The greater part of

The Divine Comedy is a catalogue of the sins of Italy' (W. B. Yeats). In seeking to make money from money itself, money-lenders had done 'violence against nature' and must now atone for it. Ezra Pound, in his 1930s 'Hell Cantos', reimagined Dante's *Inferno* as a corrupted London bank, where usurers drink 'blood sweetened with shit':

> The slough of unamiable liars,
> bog of stupidities,
> malevolent stupidities, and stupidities
> the soil living pus, full of vermin,
> dead maggots begetting live maggots,
> slum owners,
> usurers squeezing crab-lice, pandars to authority...

For Pound, as for Dante, usury was a sin against human '*arte*', which is a daughter of 'Nature': God commanded us to work and earn by the sweat of one's brow. But usury was not properly work: the Bible prohibited usury. The question was: how far could Dante's father defy the prohibition in his daily work and still carry on 'in the name of God and of profit'? Small wonder Dante nowhere mentions his father in *The Divine Comedy*; he is a ghost, a vaporized non-person. Other characters do mention him, however. Forese Donati, a sonneteer friend (who turns up in *Purgatorio*), gossiped that Dante's father was '*tra le fosse*' – 'among the pits': that is, in the Florentine debtors' prison. The Christian merchants of Florence were involved in the type of transaction that necessarily underpinned the whole capitalist enterprise – lending money at interest – and they ran the risk of spiritual dereliction. Though money-lending was a dangerous professional game, it would soon turn Florence into Europe's first financial centre, the London of its day, where the merchants were really merchant bankers, who dealt in both commodities and money, who bought and sold, accepted goods in pawn, exchanged currencies and invested in insurance.

Dante was a man who took his father-figures seriously; so his silence over his father is indicative. The most important paternal figure in the *The Divine Comedy* is not Alighiero di Bellincione, but Dante's great-great-grandfather Cacciaguida degli Elisei. Little is known historically about this figure, a Tuscan nobleman who (according to the records) was born in around 1091. It may be that Dante claimed a spurious ancestry in Cacciaguida. Though Cacciaguida came from '*poca nobilità di sangue*' ('minor noble blood'), says Dante, he was knighted by Emperor Conrad III before dying in Palestine during the second of the anti-Islamic Crusades. In claiming a Crusader ancestry for himself, Dante attempts to overcome the stigma of his usurious father. The ghost of Cacciaguida addresses Dante in *Paradiso* as his 'blood', his 'seed', 'his branch'; rarely did Dante emphasize his descent so insistently. Though Dante was not an aristocrat he wrote as though he was one. Scholars have deduced from his exaltation of Cacciaguida that he did indeed view his father as inadequate in some way. Dreadfully, 'manifest' usurers were denied Christian burial.

Alighiero was about forty-five years old when his son Dante was born; his mother, named Bella, died in childbirth some time between 1270 and 1275, when Dante was not yet in his teens. Little else is known of Bella. Dante's father soon remarried a woman named Lapa di Chiarissimo Cialuffi: another son and daughter were born. These were Francesca and Gaetano, Dante's half-siblings. In 1266, as part of his initiation into the local *societas christiana,* Dante was christened in the octagonal-shaped baptistry of San Giovanni, a Romanesque church with marble columns taken from the Forum (today the Piazza della Repubblica) of the Roman city, Florentia. The interior held works by the greatest Florentine artists of their day – mosaics, statues, tapestries, silver altar and cross and reliquaries. The church is named in honour of St John (Giovanni) the Baptist, who is the patron saint of Florence – what St Mark is to Venice or St Peter to

Rome. Built between 1059 and 1128, it is one of the oldest religious buildings in Florence, and to this day the most honoured and sacred place in the city. John was considered the last of the Hebrew prophets before the coming of Jesus. The baptistry was where, in Dante's day, the saint's relics were guarded – his jaw and two of his fingers, including the index finger that pointed to Jesus as 'the lamb of God'. Florence was thus 'the city of the Baptist' (canto 13, *Inferno*). During his years in political exile, Dante would recall with pained yearning his 'fine San Giovanni'. He hoped to be crowned there one day with a poet's laurels; it never happened. In the baptistry's cupola is a mosaic of a triple-headed demon devouring sinners in each of its three bloodied mouths. Satan is described towards the end of *Inferno* as just such a slobbering, bat-winged ogre.

Each year on 24 June – St John the Baptist's day – Dante was taken by his father to worship at San Giovanni. The Cathedral of Santa Maria del Fiore (as we know it today) had yet to be built. In pre-Renaissance Florence there was no bell tower by Giotto, no dome by Brunelleschi, no Medici palace, no Ponte Vecchio (Old Bridge) over the River Arno, and no Piazza della Signoria with its biblical David naked in marble. The Florence of Dante's boyhood was still a medieval city, with a medieval city's twisting backstreets and obscure exuberance of life. Thus, in the *Inferno*, flatterers are immersed in a ditch brimful of human excrement (not animal dung: the point is made explicitly), echoing the reality of life in Dante's Florence, where sewage drained into a reeking culvert outside the city walls. Florence was not yet the 'Italian Athens'; its architectural echoes of the Hellenic world and Florentine-Dorian marvels by da Vinci and Michelangelo began to arrive only at the fifteenth century's end. How Florence looked in Dante's day can be appreciated from a visit to nearby San Gimignano, the walled Tuscan town immortalized by E. M. Forster in his novel *Where Angels Fear to Tread*. With its seventeen surviving fortress-like towers, the town seems to float between the trees and the sky in a display of wealth and power. In canto 31 of the *Inferno* Dante mistakes a group of giants rising up from the mists of the ninth circle for 'many high towers' ('*molte alte torri*'). The towers look dark and menacing. They are in fact Satan's giant guardians, Nimrod, Ephialtes, Antaeus. Florence in Dante's day presented a vast forest of these towers. They rose over the houses, to be used for offence or defence, when the faction fights raged. Wealthy Tuscans lived in such a state of enmity with each other that they felt obliged to inhabit houses at the foot of fortified *torri*; like the inhabitants of a high-rise gated community, they looked down on the poor.

According to Dante, the Florence of his Cacciaguida was distinguished by its civic pride, probity and aristocratic civility. The baptistry marked the boundary of a close-knit, hard-working city-state. Popes and high clerics had not yet corrupted the peninsula through power and money. In *Paradiso*, Cacciaguida recalls an ancient Florence, now corrupted, which was *in pace, sobria e pudica* (at peace, sober and chaste); like a 'stately matron', this long-gone city wore no 'embroidered gown', 'gaudy sash' or 'tiara'. The inhabitants scorned makeup and jewellery. Noblemen went about in hide tunics fastened with a simple bone buckle, or else they wore unlined animal skins. Women, always 'unpainted' and therefore 'virtuous', sat contented at their spindles or, like good housewife-mothers, tending their babies. Did such a Florence ever exist? Writing in exile over thirty years on (probably in 1313, if not later), Dante is referring to an unspecified long-gone time and has conceivably fallen prey to fanciful nostalgia. It might be objected that 'nostalgia' was not in Dante's vocabulary (the term was coined in 1688), but it does seem apt: from the Greek *nostos* and *algos,* 'a painful yearning to return home', nostalgia might be

The Baptistery of San Giovanni, one of the oldest buildings in Florence, where Dante was baptised in 1266; the baptistery – 'my beautiful San Giovanni' – is mentioned in *The Divine Comedy.*

overleaf   Detail from the thirteenth-century ceiling mosaic of the Baptistery of San Giovanni, *The Last Judgement*, showing Satan, with serpents protruding, eating three damned souls. The mosaic influenced Dante's portrayal of Satan.

excused in an exile whose tendency to exaggerate was a poet's right. As a Tuscan proverb has it: 'The tale is not beautiful if nothing has been added to it.'

Florence in Dante's day was an independent republic ruled by the church on one side, and by trade guilds on the other. It was one of the most populous cities on the peninsula; only Milan, Venice and Genoa could equal its 100,000-strong population. The trade guilds were organized into miniature republics, each with its own officers, councils and heraldic banner-bearers. The so-called *Arti Maggiori* or Greater Guilds were represented by lawyers, bankers, doctors, merchants and other 'professionals'. They were entrusted with the city's governance proper. A total of six Greater Guild members – one for each of the six *sestieri* of Florence – were appointed senators or 'priors'. In order to avoid the possibility of dictatorship, these priors could hold office only for two months. A so-called *Gonfaloniere* or 'Standard-bearer of Justice' was appointed to restrain and balance any tendency towards the abuse of power. The Lesser Guilds or *Arti Minori* were represented by craftsmen, tradesmen and woollen-industry labourers. Together the Greater and Lesser guilds represented the *popolo* – not the 'people' as understood in a modern democracy but what we might think of, rather, as the bourgeoisie. The *popolo* was that part of Florence in opposition to the interests of the old powerful families or feudal magnates, simply called the *grandi* (big shots). Before long Dante would be appointed a prior; but, as we shall see, it was senatorial ambition that led to his political downfall and exile.

In reality, Florence was a republic in name only. Rival factions and rival families manipulated politics and alliances to extend their power in monarchic fashion. The feudal stone towers spoke of clan violence and other dark vested interests. Tuscan towns were built on family allegiances and the *cultura dell'appartenenza* – the mentality that seeks strength in a feeling of belonging. It was a matter of duty for a noble Florentine to avenge an insult with violence. 'A 100-year vendetta keeps you as young as a child at the mother's breast', ran a Florentine proverb. Revenge was not simply an act of justice; it was a means of preserving personal honour. Public executions were common in mid-to-late-thirteenth-century Florence. Dante said he saw people burned at the stake in front of jeering crowds. He was in direct view of the pyre and only a child at the time.

Childhood is conspicuously absent from medieval literature, and Dante makes scarce mention of it in his own writing. We can assume that he began his formal education at around the age of six. As the Alighieri family lacked the funds to appoint a private tutor, in the early 1270s Dante was sent to a municipal-run school that taught grammar (that is, Latin), along with logic, rhetoric, arithmetic, geometry and music. With later study he became proficient in the classics and could read Ovid, Virgil, Lucan and Cicero. His earliest grammar book was thought to have been *Ars Grammatica* by the fourth-century grammarian Aelius Donatus, whose soul Dante would place among the learned in *Paradiso*. Instruction was mostly in the Florentine vernacular. The language of Florentine daily life enabled Dante to make headway in understanding Latin ('enter Latin', he put it), and set him on 'the path of knowledge'. While Dante would recognize the importance of 'Latinity', as a young man his formal education in Latin was barely sufficient to decipher formulaic Latin legal documents. Dante would have been able to manipulate basic sequences of words in Latin and translate them, but not much more. Later, by the time Dante came to write the *Vita nuova*, he had become a formidable 'man of letters', who had studied Latin grammar and prosody, and gained a deep understanding of Classical literary works.

overleaf
Illustration of Florence from the 1493 Nuremberg Chronicle, an early printed book or *incunabulum*. Note the fortified castle walls and the bridges over the River Arno.

*

Florence was a city full of wealth: 'like Rome', declares a 1255 inscription on the wall of the Palazzo del Bargello, 'she is ever triumphant'. Beneath the roseate flush of florin-prosperity, however, lay a deepening political unease. Dante's childhood was marked by the centuries-old struggle between the Italian papacy and the Holy Roman Empire. In Florence the struggle was fought between two aristocratic factions known as the Guelfs and Ghibellines. Put simply, the Guelfs favoured the pope, and the Ghibellines the emperor. Each faction laid claim to the allegiance of the Italian peninsula's numerous feudal lords and city-states (*comuni*), as well as to the emperor as the titular head of secular power in Europe and the pope as the head of Western Christendom. It did not take much for a personal or family feud to become part of a larger feud identified with the antagonism between Guelfs and Ghibellines. Since neither the pope nor the emperor could exert significant control from afar, their rivalry was played out on the streets of Florence, and between Florence and other Tuscan towns: Siena, Lucca, Pistoia. If a large Tuscan city was Guelf, the smaller cities around it were likely to be Ghibelline, implicitly appealing for protection from afar. It may be that many at the time in Florence, including possibly the young Dante, found it hard to know what was really going on, apart from fighting. Max Beerbohm's humorous 1919 tale '*Savonarola' Brown* contains, time and again and for no particular reason, the stage direction 'Enter Guelfs and Ghibellines, fighting', followed after a while by '*Exeunt* Guelfs and Ghibellines, still fighting'.

Though the Guelfs were in favour of the pope, they were not very much in favour of him. Of course the pope should have power, but not an excess of it. The Guelfs tended to dominate where people felt they had more to fear from the German-based Holy Roman Emperor than from the Holy See. It was the party of the nouveaux riches: bankers, traders, anyone who had an interest in the formation of a looser, less rigidly controlled Florentine republic. The Ghibellines, by contrast, attracted those who stood to benefit from the hierarchical structures of feudalism, or who simply felt uncomfortably close to a papal state set on territorial expansion.

In some ways, of course, this is too neat. As recent Italian history has shown, Italian politics have an infinite capacity for *fibrillazione* or splintering. Thus it would not be long before the Guelfs were fighting among themselves, and the Ghibellines were showing Guelfic tendencies. The truth is, neither party had a stable hold on people's identity: divisions over commercial, religious and family issues often blurred black-and-white allegiances. And, in spite of Guelf propaganda that their opponents were heretical, most Ghibellines acknowledged the spiritual authority of the church. What they objected to was papal intrusion into the temporal realm and the popes' determination to replace the power of the Hohenstaufen (Holy Roman Empire) dynasty with a French kingdom in southern Italy.

Officially, the Alighieri family were Guelfs, but they cannot have been especially grand Guelfs. Five years before Dante's birth, in 1260, the Tuscan Ghibellines prevailed at the battle of Montaperti near Siena. A mass expulsion from Florence of all Guelfs followed. The triumphant Ghibellines, having threatened to raze Florence to the ground, instead demolished 100 Guelf *palazzi*, 600 Guelf houses and 90 Guelf towers. If Dante's father was allowed to stay on in Florence (and his house saved from demolition), it was because he was not considered socially significant enough for exile. The Ghibellines' control of Florence anyway lasted no more than six years. The Holy Roman Emperor Frederick II's son Manfred, a Ghibelline stalwart, was defeated in battle by Charles of Anjou at Benevento in southern Italy in 1266. With the help of loans from exiled Florentine Guelf bankers,

Charles helped the Guelfs to reclaim power in Florence and exact revenge on any remaining Ghibellines. The whole of southern and central Italy, Sicily and Tuscany (where Charles assumed the title of imperial vicar) were now under Guelf control.

The Guelfs remained uneasily dominant in Florence throughout Dante's childhood. Dante's family kept on the right side of Guelf power through systems of patronage; they knew they had to side with family friends, and with the friends of those friends, if they were to stave off the common Ghibelline enemy, and not be foiled and overthrown. Rarely has a politico-economic feud involved such in-fighting. The memory of Guelf–Ghibelline discord lingers even today in Italy. In his 1945 memoir of internal exile under Mussolini, *Christ Stopped at Eboli*, the Turinese painter and medical doctor Carlo Levi (no relation to Primo Levi) compared the southern Italian peasants of remote Gagliano (Aliano) to the pro-church Guelfs, and the gentry of Gagliano to the pro-feudal Ghibellines. Never making friends but only foes, the factions were at loggerheads perenially.

Dante's father was able to maintain his family in some comfort through his financial dealings. He sought out business connections (in current Italian, *raccomandazioni*) with Florentine merchant-banker families such as the Peruzzi and the Bardi, whose business stretched across Europe from Sicily to London. At the dawn of the fourteenth century political power in Florence rested increasingly in the hands of great banking families. Banking (from the Italian word *banco*, 'counter') was essentially Florentine in origin. Dante was not against money. But, as he later saw it, greed led to the search for profit and then to fraud. To an extent, his animus against bankers and merchants was borne out by history. The Medici Bank, founded in Florence in 1397, would operate like a prototype mafia consortium; it disposed of great wealth and spread its tentacles into what Niccolò Machiavelli called the *alti luoghi* ('high places') of local power interests, tight-bound networks of kinship and marriage. Officially this web of personal relationships acted to cut down on chicanery, but it also meant that bad faith in business, when it occurred, often amounted to a much deeper, more personal degree of betrayal. Through boom and bust, the banking class of Florence amassed its towering wealth by means of a twenty-four-carat gold coin introduced in 1252, a decade before Dante's birth, called the florin or *fiorino*. The florin took its name, like Florence itself, from the word for flower, *fiore* in Tuscan vernacular. How much was the florin worth? One florin is thought to be equivalent to between 100 and 150 euros in today's money: about £110. In Dante's day, a slave girl – or a mule – could be bought for fifty florins, about £5,500.

One florin weighed roughly 3.53 grammes of pure gold. On one side of the new gold coin was the lily, emblem of Florence, and on the other St John the Baptist. At the behest of civic leaders and merchant bankers (often the same men), municipal pride and religious observance were thus conveniently fused – in gold. Until 1237, when Florence set up a mint and struck the silver florin, the town had been using the *denaro* of the declining Holy Roman Empire, but the coin had become debased. The American dollar of its time, the florin was a transnational currency known in England as a 'florence'. By the end of the thirteenth century, the florin was used in commercial transactions all over Europe. It was a coin for serious trade. Inevitably in Dante's Florence it was becoming more important to monetize all transactions and transform all wealth into money. To what end? Once Florentines were permitted to play with florins, lend them, multiply them, have them 'copulate' and reproduce, they would have little time left for God and more for Mammon. Florins, Dante wrote later, were an 'accursed flower' (*maladetto fiore*) that blossomed from the interests of those who put profit before morals.

On 9 January 1277, barely twelve years old, Dante was betrothed to a child of the Donati banking family, called Gemma, who was presumably even younger than he. The prenuptial negotiations resulted in one known document, signed in the presence of witnesses and the notary on 9 February, in which a dowry of 200 small florins or *fiorini piccoli* was settled, the equivalent of just over 125 gold florins: about £13,750 in today's terms, a respectable if not a huge amount of money for socially elevated families at that time in Florence. Like most medieval matrimonies, Dante's was celebrated at the bride's home, not in church. The notary would have united the couple 'in the name of the Holy Trinity, the Father, Son and Holy Spirit, of the glorious Virgin Mary, and the entire celestial court'. The dowry is among the first known documentary evidence of Dante's existence. Childhood betrothals of this sort were not uncommon in the late Italo-Christian Middle Ages. They were designed to secure a good dowry and elevate a family's social rank. As young adolescents (in Latin, *impuberes*), Dante and Gemma had not yet reached the legal age of adults, which was twelve for females, and fourteen for males. Their respective families had affected a matrimonial alliance, but the marriage proper would not be consummated until a dozen years later, in around 1283 or 1285. (In Dante's day, men did not marry, on average, until they were thirty; women were usually fifteen.)

The Donatis, supremely political animals within the Florentine Guelf faction, had obtained their pre-eminence through a dense capillary network of clients, contacts and society marriages. Eight years or so later, probably in 1285, Dante and Gemma were married. They were to have four children, all born before Dante was sent into exile: Giovanni, Pietro, Jacopo, Antonia. We know very little about these children (though Antonia became a nun with the name Beatrice). Just as Dante never wrote of his childhood, so he never wrote about his wife and family. Most of our information comes from Dante's first biographer, Giovanni Boccaccio, who tells us that Dante was a 'lustful' man even in middle age and that his marriage brought him only strife. Boccaccio concludes sagely that such is the fate of all men of genius (*filosofanti*) who marry. In fact, Dante's marriage was probably no worse than any other marriage; the problem for his wife Gemma would be that Dante had given himself in his imagination to another woman, whose 'flower-soft' alien loveliness put Gemma in the shade. And this woman, incredibly, had entered Dante's life long before the betrothal was arranged for him in 1277.

Dante called
her Beatrice

If we are to believe Dante, Beatrice was encountered by him for the first time in 1274 when he was just nine, and she eight. The meeting was described by Dante in his first book, *La Vita nuova* (*The New Life*), completed in the mid-1290s following Beatrice's death. The girl, in appearance a 'young angel', was wearing a dress of 'a modest proper crimson'; crimson, the colour of love and nobility, was thought also to symbolize the blood of Christ's redeeming sacrifice. Her complexion was pearl-like (but not, Dante stresses, pale to excess). Lightbeams appeared to glitter from her eyes. In *Purgatorio* those eyes are compared to intense burning green *smeraldi* (emeralds). Beatrice was devout and, it was said, profoundly venerated the Virgin Mary. The meeting was an intoxicating rapture for Dante; he did not know it then, but it was the central and determining episode of his young life.

Beatrice's father, the Guelf banker Folco Portinari, had invited Dante and family members to a party celebrating the coming of spring. The Portinari, who lived at the higher altitude of Florentine society, had spared no expense in making garlands and wreaths of woodbine and hawthorn. It was 1 May and the time of year was propitious for Dante. May is the Virgin Mary's month; in the *Vita nuova* Beatrice is described in Marian terms of renewal and nature's motherhood. From the earliest pages of that book, words such as *meraviglia* (marvellous), *miracolo* (miracle) and *mirare* (wonder) indicate that Beatrice is Holy Beatrix, the bringer of blessedness, with echoes too of Christ as *salus nostra*, 'our salvation'. Christ appears only fleetingly in Dante's writing (he was a Christian writer who largely ignored Christ); instead, Beatrice takes on the mantle of saviour.

Girdled with May flowers, Beatrice seemed to be something like perfection to the boy Dante. Perhaps, in some unformulated way, he understood already that Beatrice was to have a salvific purpose for him. Later, in the *The Divine Comedy*, Dante will stake his very moral fate on the miracle woman. The poem effectively hinges on Beatrice as a seraph-like purifying angel. She is the one who will transform *amor* (love) into *caritas* (Christian love of humankind). To the cynically minded, the power she exerts over Dante as a child is a nonsense. All it took was one look at the crimson-dressed apparition for Dante to fall headlong and helplessly in love. The feeling was so intense, apparently, that it convulsed his body like a 'painful illness'; he almost died of love.

> At that moment, and I speak the truth, the vital spirit, the one that dwells in the most secret chamber of my heart, began to tremble so violently that even the tiniest veins of my body were strangely affected; and, trembling, it spoke these words: *Ecce deus fortiori me, qui veniens dominabitur mihi.*

'Here is a god stronger than I am, who comes to rule over me.' With these Latin words – the august language meant to convey the authority of his new master, Love – Dante proclaims Beatrice's domination of his heart. The first stirrings of puberty may have accounted for the frenzy-spasms he suffered. Beatrice was no sooner born than she caused Dante to fall to the ground as if his 'little childish body' had been struck by lightning. So Dante claimed; but, as Dante was then only a baby of nine months, this seems unlikely. Rather, Dante's claim in later life that Beatrice was his one and only love ('always and only the praise of the gracious Beatrice') was part of his self-portrayal as someone exceptional: a visionary poet in the making.

Dante discloses Beatrice's name several times in his work (occasionally in the abbreviated form 'Bice'); from the start, she was a real-life woman, who provoked long-drawn-out moans and sighs. After that spring encounter, Dante saw Beatrice on a number of occasions. A casual greeting, an exchange of looks, at most a few words; it was not until Dante was eighteen that Beatrice spoke to him at length. The year was 1282. By now Beatrice had married the aristocratic financier Simone dei Bardi; consequently

E CUI SALUTA, FA TREMAR LO CORE

IL SALŪ

Il salute di Beatrice (Beatrice's salutation) by Dante Gabriel Rossetti.
The 1849–50 ink drawing shows Dante's muse as a young woman in
the *Vita nuova* and at the end of *Purgatorio*.

GUARDAMI BEN; BEN SON, BEN SON BEATRICE

BEATRICE

she stood on a much higher social ledge than Dante, making him perhaps jealous. Beatrice was dressed this time in angelic 'purest white', no longer in blood red. She was walking in Florence with two older women. Words were exchanged; Dante was rewarded with a smile. Buoyed by her enthusiastic glance in his direction he began to write sensuous, impassioned 'rhymes of love'. The poetry so occupied him that he lost all sense of danger, how love might crush the life out of him. One night he became aware of a fiery presence watching by his bed, its shadow scalding and oppressive. The creature said its name was Love; it had come to Dante in a dream. This intimidating, fire-shrouded figure appeared to be holding Beatrice semi-naked and asleep in his arms. Worse still, he was brandishing something wreathed in flames. '*Vide cor tuum*', Love announced to Dante. 'Behold your heart.' Beatrice stirred and, grossly enraptured, ate the burning heart, which of course was Dante's heart. Afterwards Love gathered up Beatrice and ascended with her towards heaven. What could it all mean? And why was Beatrice a participant in such horror? The dream did not so such much clarify Dante's thoughts as drive them deeper into puzzlement and, before long, despair. W. B. Yeats, who fell under the influence of Dante through Rossetti's English translations, was so transfixed by this vision of the fiery heart that he wrote a poem about it, 'Ego Dominus Tuus', where Beatrice is described as 'The most exalted Lady loved by a man'.

*

Some days later, Dante again caught sight of Beatrice. She was seated this time in a city church, perhaps the baptistry of San Giovanni. Once more Dante was overwhelmed by the presence of this 'most courtly lady', who set off palpitations in his heart and made him pallid and weak. Dante tried to conceal his crazy, blind-groping love but gossip reached Beatrice who, on their next

meeting, cut her lover dead in public. Her cold averted eyes –
the unexpected snub – devastated Dante, who fled to his room
as usual and moped on his bed like a 'little child that had been
beaten'. His disturbed mental state and exhausted, spectrally
white face were plain to all Florentine high society. ('See how that
lady makes him waste away?') At a marriage feast, Beatrice joined
other women in mocking the sudden weakness that seemed to
overwhelm Dante at the sight of her. 'Since you end up by looking
so ridiculous whenever you are near this lady, why do you keep
trying to see her?' the women chorused. Dante had no strength to
say anything; Beatrice sent him shuddering back to bed.

Sightings of Beatrice ('she who gives everybody beatitude')
continued to provoke feelings of ecstasy combined with anxiety
in Dante. He began to fall ill, sometimes very ill, afflicted by a
'painful disease' that confined him to his room for days on
end. A teenage crush? Youth's hot prime at work? There are
sufficient grounds to wonder if Dante was not marked by some
sort of chronic condition. One moment he is upright, the next
in bed as if inebriated. A long line of geniuses have suffered
from what the ancients called the 'falling sickness', among them
Dostoevsky, Graham Greene, Emily Dickinson, Edward Lear,
George Gershwin and, it seems likely, Joan of Arc. The epileptic
was seen as someone set apart and subject to inscrutable, other-
worldly afflictions. A more recent epileptic, Ian Curtis of the
Manchester New Wave band Joy Division, was thought to mimic
the condition's convulsive onset in his jerky, spasmodic dance
routines. ('She's Lost Control', the band's fear-ridden hosanna to
the disorder, was oddly not included on the Joy Division bootleg
album *Dante's Inferno*, released in Italy in 1985.) What was it that
so drained Dante of his strength and left him stunned, hopeless, if
not a tendency for his brain to fire, as it were, abnormally?

Cesare Lombroso, the 'criminal' anthropologist who operat-
ed out of nineteenth-century Turin, was convinced of Dante's ep-

ilepsy. Dante's seizures blotted out the light and were life-devouring. According to Dante's latest biographer, Marco Santagata, Lombroso's theory has never really been accepted by scholars, but after catching sight of Beatrice the young Dante did at times seem to be in *status epilepticus*. In the *Vita nuova* he is often so 'pallid and void of strength' that he is left 'immobile', like those 'who are paralysed'. The 'fainting pallor' of Dante's face suggests a man in considerable torment. A 'tremor began on the left side of my body', he writes. From the Greek 'to capture' or 'to seize', epilepsy was associated in Italy in the Middle Ages with black magic, demonic possession, visitations from the Beyond. There was a widely held view – expressed by the twelfth-century mystic-anchorite Hildegard of Bingen – that the devil acted on a susceptible body through the 'breath of his power of suggestion' (*flatu suggestionis suae*). Those who suffered epilepsy brought shame on themselves and their kin; yet, far from attenuating the diabolical aura of the disorder, Dante presents it in the *Vita nuova* as something predestined and exceptional, says his biographer Santagata.

Dante was not merely self-obsessed but self-inventive. Among all the versifiers of his medieval century, Dante alone had received the gift of love's affliction (*amor hereos*). Whether epilepsy really lay behind Dante's sense of a poetic purpose is impossible to say. But, though drained by the seizures, Dante felt grandly blessed by them. A similar, psycho-physical crisis to Dante's occurs in canto 24 of the *Inferno*, where a petty Guelf bully and gangster, Vanni Fucci, is restored to human form after a serpent has reduced him to ashes after a bite from its venomed fang:

> Just as a man who falls, not knowing why –
> forced by a demon who hauls him down to earth
> or by some other oppilation that holds him down –
> will struggle to his feet and look around him
> confused and overwhelmed by the great anguish
> he has suffered, moaning as he stares about –
> just so this sinner, when finally on his feet again.

Dante's use of the Latinate technical term 'oppilation' (*oppilazion*), meaning 'obstruction', 'blockage' or 'snare', suggests a familiarity with the medieval medical word for an excess of bodily humours that clogged or 'oppilated' the brain, leading to epilepsy. Dante's tendency to faint whenever love 'assails' him makes sense as in canto 5 of the *Inferno*, the episode dominated by Francesca's love for Paolo, Dante says of himself 'I fell as a dead body falls' (*'e caddi come corpo morto cade'*); like a heavy lifeless thing he falls to the ground.

*

Florence had no university in Dante's day. Instead religious foundations – particularly the mendicant orders – played a significant part in educational life. Probably Dante took part in 'whatever pleases' (*'quodlibetal'*) disputations held in public in the mendicant houses of Santa Maria Novella and Santa Croce. Florentine citizens were invited to question Dominican and Franciscan friars on the finer points of theology and philosophy. (Lists of questions asked by Dante's contemporaries on the nature of sin have survived.) Scholastic disputation of this sort, which considered quasi-philosophical questions of knowledge, the nature of time and the role of language, encouraged a habit of argument in Dante. Dante's great lay mentor was Brunetto Latini, a notary and intransigent Guelf, who was among the first in the Middle Ages to urge a return to Greco-Roman culture, thus paving the way for what became the European Renaissance. Very little is known about the practicalities of Latini's instruction – was it conducted at home? in public? – but it was a lasting and formative influence. Forty-five years older than Dante, Latini was renowned for his skill as a political and civil public speaker. He espoused the writings of the Latin orator Cicero and taught Dante the rudiments of Latin prose rhetoric. For reasons known only to Dante, Latini appears in the seventh circle of Hell of the *Inferno*

GVIDO CAVAL
CANT

reserved for 'sinners against nature', among them homosexuals. In the charred and fatty air Latini cuts a wretched yet oddly dignified figure; though damned, he muses proudly on his past as a scholar and man of letters.

Young Dante's other shaping influence was the poet-aristocrat Guido Cavalcanti. Like Dante, Cavalcanti was a Guelf allied to pro-papal factions in Florence. Admired by Ezra Pound, Cavalcanti's was a dryly philosophical if often witty vernacular verse that derived in part from the Provençal tradition of the troubadours. Cavalcanti was an Averroist (what in modern terms we would call an atheist). In crystal language he spoke of love as a lacerating illness that elevated the soul but destroyed the body. The troubadour poetry of chivalric knights and their idealized love had become popular at the courts of Europe when knights went on pilgrimage to the Holy Land, leaving behind and pining for their women. Cavalcanti was aware of predecessor poets from twelfth-century Languedoc, but his verse was far more scholastic and sombrous than anything by the troubadours. Indeed it rejected the *trobar clus* (closed form) of Provençal courtly verse; the most disquieting emotional experiences were discussed by Cavalcanti in difficult rhythms, disjunctive syntax and grating sonorities. It is difficult to talk about a Cavalcantian school but in *The Divine Comedy* Dante gives it the name '*dolce stil novo*', or 'sweet new style', in deference to its euphony and refined lexicon. Whether such a school ever existed outside Dante's fantasy (and his biased literary history) is debatable. Over the last three decades scholars have tended to exclude it. Perhaps, in coining the term *dolce stil novo*, Dante had simply wanted to be credited with founding a new poetry movement. However, the fact that we continue to refer to *dolce stil novo* is proof of Dante's influence as an author and literary critic. (In old Italian, incidentally, *dolce* is a much more forceful word than 'sweet' and lacks any cloying or saccharine associations.)

Early seventeenth-century oil portrait of Dante's poet friend (and, later, enemy) Guido Cavalcanti by the Bolognese artist Antonio Maria Crespi.

Dante's own career as a writer of vernacular verse – roughly, from the early 1280s to the mid-1290s – was inseparable from the example set by the older Florentine poet Cavalcanti. The *Vita nuova* was dedicated to Cavalcanti, and in time Cavalcanti would become Dante's *primo amico* or best friend, as Dante called him. The endearment was revived by T. S. Eliot, who, in a letter to Ezra Pound of 1925, addresses his older poet friend as his '*mio primo amico*', after Cavalcanti.

The *stilnovist* verse of Cavalcanti and others was rooted in late medieval Sicily, where the emperor-king Frederick II had patronized a group of courtier-poets. From around 1233 they began to write traditional Provençal troubadour verse in a new literary language: the Sicilian vernacular. The vernacular was not unlike the Sicilian vernacular of today; to the pride of many Sicilians, Italian was thus first established as a literary language in Sicily. The language of the Sicilian poets – a Sicilian version of the Romance vernacular – became a point of reference for Dante as he developed the Tuscan language. All Italian poetry was in Dante's youth referred to as 'Sicilian'. It was Sicilian, or at least southern Italian in origin, character and expression. Scholars have debated how much of a Saracen influence shows in the verse. The Arabs invaded Sicily in the ninth century, leaving behind mosques, pink-domed cupolas, and a few thousand verses by Siculo-Arabic poet-panegyrists, among them the great Ibn Hamdis. The Sicilian capital of Palermo, where Frederick II held court between 1220 and 1250, was far removed from the gracious suavities of pre-Renaissance Florence. Jasmine-flavoured ice and sherbet was served as refreshment after the sirocco had blown in hot and sandy from Tunisia. It was the Arabs who brought sherbet to this part of the Mediterranean – jasmine is surely a Saracen touch. Sicilian vulgate poets such as Giacomo da Lentini, Ciullo d'Alcamo, Rinaldo d'Aquino – all of them mentioned in *The Divine Comedy* – wrote for an exclusive audience at Frederick's palace; only Sicilians of refinement (and, of course, leisure) could enjoy their mannered, antiquarian verse. Dante Gabriel Rossetti translated a selection of it for his 1861 volume *The Early Italian Poets from Ciullo d'Alcamo to Dante Alighieri*, a high point of literary Pre-Raphaelitism. Sicilian verse was haunted by two and a half centuries of Arabic culture; d'Alcamo and his peers enjoyed falconry, chess, checkers, and backgammon; they wrote of date palms, cloisters, turban-wearing pashas, tresses of golden hair, perfumed roses, sultans, minarets, concubines, *zajal* and *muwashshah* songs and other music played on the Arabic lute and tambourine. Alcamo, as Rossetti acknowledged in a footnote, took his Arabic name from Alcamo town outside Palermo, which has an Arabic fortress.

We know of the existence of more than 170 Siculo-Arabic poets at work in Sicily before the Normans came to oust the Arabs in the eleventh century. Inevitably their poetry stood as a model – attractive, unavoidable – for the first Italian troubadour poets who were to influence Dante. Ibn Hamdis, the greatest of the Arabic Sicilian poets, had taken part in attacks against the invading Normans before emigrating to Seville. Scholars have found traces of Hamdis-style Arabic sonorities and elements of Islamic lyric tradition in both d'Alcamo's use of sibilance and alliteration ('*rosa fresca aulentissima*', 'sweetly-smelling fresh red rose') and in the way he divines a trace of the astrological moon in the face of his *donna amata* (beloved woman). The poetry, much of it, reads like a lost leaf out of some early *Arabian Nights*, and traces of it will insinuate their way into Dante's work.

From the Sicilian poets Dante acquired an idea of courtly love poetry or *fin amor* (refined love). This which spoke of an unconsummated passion for an idealized distant woman, and the troubadour-Provençal motif of illicit romance. Dante later condemned emperor-king Frederick to the fiery tombs of the heretics in canto 10 of the *Inferno* (his fostering of Islamic culture displeased Christendom; the pope excommunicated him). At this early stage of his writing life, however, Dante praised Frederick as a paragon of chivalric virtue. A Renaissance prince before his time, Frederick had written a manual on the Arabic art of falconry, and commissioned Latin translations of the great Arab philosopher and interpreter of Aristotle, Averroës. Frederick was a poet, too.

Such was the power of Provençalism among the 'Sicilian school' that Dante is said to have considered writing *The Divine Comedy* in Siculo-Provençal rather than in Tuscan. The Sicilian dialect poets had invented the two most important forms of Italian verse: the *canzone* (from the Provençal *canso*), a lyric poem suited to a musical setting, and the sonnet, a strictly rhymed fourteen-line poem. It is curious to reflect that sonnets by Milton and Shakespeare 'originated' on an island which many Italians regard as shrouded in an African darkness – the place where Europe finally ends. (A smug joke still told in northern Italy is that Sicily is the only Arab country not at war with Israel.) On Frederick's death in 1250, the new Sicilian poetry migrated to peninsular Italy, first to the north and then south to Tuscany, where it was firmly established by the time Dante was starting to write. Inevitably the poetry lost something, in transit, of its original vigour and tinge of Saracen exoticism.

The most prominent of the Tuscan followers of the Sicilian school, Guittone d'Arezzo, was known for his dizzying feats of rhetorical virtuosity, smart repartee and pyrotechnics of rhyme and metre. Dante's first love lyrics, with their literary flavour of joust and jest, showed a marked Tuscan-Provençal influence as filtered through d'Arezzo. Lyrics by d'Arezzo belonged to a courtly world where honour and nobility were all. Even his political poem '*Ahi, lasso!*', written after the Florentine Guelf defeat at Montaperti in 1260 ('Ah, alas! How long does so much misery last?'), seemed to put stylistic virtuosity before emotion. Dante would soon react against d'Arezzo's verse as being excessively ostentatious and hyperbolic. Even in his late teens, Dante had ambitions to turn Italian into a vehicle for a higher and much more serious poetry.

He found an element of the seriousness he was looking for in the Bologna-born poet Guido Guinizzelli. To Dante, Guinizzelli was *il saggio* (the wise man) of vernacular love poetry. Guinizzelli's celebrated poem 'Al cor gentil' ('Love always comes to the noble heart') is regarded as the founding work of the *dolce stil novo* movement. The *canzone*'s insistence on the nobility of heart – only the noble-hearted can truly love – was a theme that Dante would explore later in his own prose works. In his verse, Guinizzelli sees the desired woman as a semi-angelic vehicle of beatitude and love itself as a transcendent power. This was not exactly new, but Guinizzelli's analysis of the psychology of love was different in kind to all poetry that had gone before. What is this thing called love? The ever-burning question exercised the younger generation of Florentine *stilnovist* poets to which Dante would soon belong.

From Guinizzelli, later *stilnovist* poets such as Cavalcanti inherited not just a tone of restlessly inquiring psychology but an extreme clarity of diction – what Ezra Pound, in his great 1912 essay on Cavalcanti, called 'the medieval clean line'. Cavalcanti's magnificent poem 'Donna me prega' ('A Woman Asks Me'), written in *dialetto toscano*, profoundly influenced Dante. In a series of highly wrought, slyly humorous lines, Cavalcanti contemplates the destructive passion of love, which leaves the wounded suitor bereft of reason. Love hurts. If you love, you are doomed to a life of suffering if not mental disarray. Ezra Pound offered a typically antiquarian translation of Cavalcanti's poem, where love is seen as 'an accident' that flails destructively out of hand.

Because a lady asks me, I would tell
Of an affect that comes often and is fell
And is so overweening; Love by name.

So what is love? For Cavalcanti, love brings only blindness and *tristitia* (melancholy). Dante's own answer to the question will surface in the *Vita nuova*. And the answer is Beatrice.

*

Aflame with ambition, in 1286 Dante circulated among the leading *stilnovist* poets of Florence a fourteen-line poem about his dream of Beatrice consuming the burning heart. Manuscript circulation was a common form of publication in the days before printing, when books were few and expensive. Dante, who was not quite twenty, displayed in his sonnet a frequently clumsy rhetoric and trite repetition of the lover's hopes and fears. D'Arezzo's influence showed in the hyperbolic overture to 'Joyous Love' and sense of a wildly writhing torment. Most of the Florentine poets who received the sonnet claimed not to be able to understand it (one, a doctor, advised his 'rather dim friend' Dante to wash his testicles in cold water in order to calm himself). Cavalcanti, however, understood it, and responded immediately with a sonnet of his own: 'I think that you beheld all goodness' in that vision of the burning heart, he wrote to Dante: Beatrice eating the heart signified that Dante's whole life was destined to be consumed by his love for her. The heart, in medieval literature, was seen as love's mansion and the physiological centre of the human being. With Cavalcanti's accolade, Dante's career as a Florentine vernacular poet had begun. From then on nothing he wrote could be ignored. He tried his hand at ever more refined sonnets and *canzoni* that expressed a sorrowful, Cavalcantian sense of the suffering imposed by love. He and Cavalcanti began to exchange poems, some of them quite boyish, on that vexing subject of love.

The poet Peter Hughes, in his inventive 2017 collection *Cavalcanty* (the misspelling is intentional), re-interprets one such poem:

> Hi Dantz – hope you're not partying too hard
> I was going to send you these poems
> about my heart going through the juicer
> when love looking like death smashed down the door
> shouting: 'stop – don't be such an idiot!'

*

Lovelorn, sore and chagrined, Dante was out walking in Florence one day when he decided to address a poem about Beatrice to '*Donne ch'avete intelletto d'amore*' ('Women who understand the truth of love'). The poem was a signpost in Dante's development as a writer and, incidentally, a pinnacle of the European love lyric. That Dante chose to address the poem to women, rather than to the usual male audience, suggests that he now saw women as more than merely beautiful bodies. In his mind, love and vernacular poetry were intimately involved, therefore his 'dear dames and damozels' ought to be able to understand and read the poem. The poem's theme – the praise of Beatrice – initiated a new sweet style of poetry, in which Love's universe is conceived as encompassing the whole of humankind, not just a sole lovelorn suitor. The contemporary New York poet Andrew Frisardi translated the opening lines:

> Women who understand the truth of love,
> I want to talk with you a while about
> my lady – not because I could run out
> of words and ways to praise her, but to set
> my mind at ease. Her worth is so above
> the rest, I feel such lightness in my heart,
> that if speech didn't stammer I'd impart
> new love to those who are not lovers yet.

Dante was so proud of this poem that he put it at the very centre of the *Vita nuova* and, a quarter of a century after that, quotes the first line in canto 24 of *Purgatorio* as an outstanding example (in his view) of *dolce stil novo* verse; the poem made his name in Florence.

*

Politics intruded on Dante during this great Beatrician period. In 1289, having been trained in horsemanship and the use of the lance, the twenty-four-year-old poet fought in the first rank of the Florentine cavalry against the Ghibellines at the Battle of Campaldino. The battle was the culmination of a long-drawn-out brutal campaign. Earlier, Dante had witnessed the posthumous trial in Florence of the Ghibelline leader Farinata degli Uberti (who died in 1264); having been declared a heretic, he was exhumed and his body ceremonially burned at the stake. That would not be the end of him. Two decades later Farinata rose up before Dante from an open tomb in *Inferno*. Ghibelline and Guelf were locked eyeball to eyeball in Hell, amid the flames of heresy:

> My gaze was already fixed on his
> and he rose upwards with his chest and forehead
> as if he thought of Hell with great scorn.

The battle of Campaldino won, the Guelfs were now in control of Florence. Unfortunately they lost little time in dividing themselves into two new factions: the Black Guelfs and the White Guelfs. Nominally the Blacks were more favourable to the interests of the old noble class, and the Whites more aligned with the rising merchant class. The old, pro-papal Guelf versus pro-imperial Ghibelline political ideologies had vanished; motivated chiefly by power and money-lust, the new Black–White antagonism was as ferocious as it was mindless. Very soon there was hardly a family in Florence, noble or plebian,

Farinata degli Uberti rising from his tomb in canto 10 of the *Inferno*. Gustave Doré's illustration shows Dante walking with Virgil among the burning tombs of the Heretics.

that was not divided against itself. Seamus Heaney, in his poetry collection *Station Island*, compared the tragic political landscape of Northern Ireland (Protestant 'Orange bigots' versus Catholic 'hard-mouthed bigots') to the implacable hatred of Guelf versus Guelf – and Guelf versus Ghibelline. 'Farinata rising out of the tomb could be Ian Paisley', the Northern Irish poet said of the loyalist preacher-politician.

Dante backed the White Guelfs, even though his wife Gemma Donati was related to the leader of the Black Guelfs, the terrifying and thuggish Corso Donati. Dante had married Gemma shortly after the death of his father in 1283. All four of their children were to suffer at the hands of the Black Guelfs, with Dante himself exiled by them. Dante was ruined by his wife's family, yet he refrains from placing Corso Donati in the *Inferno*, leaving it to his brother Forese Donati, a *stilnovist* poet, to describe Corso's grisly death as he was dragged by a beast to Hell.

*

Dante's world now collapsed. On 8 June 1290, a year after the Battle of Campaldino, Beatrice died. She was twenty-four. All vitality left Dante; he felt obliterated. Through bitter-sad tears he looked up to heaven to see a multitude of angels 'returning upwards' while chanting *Hosanna in excelsis*. The words 'Hosanna in the highest' (Mark 11:10) had marked Christ's triumphal entry into Jerusalem; here they imply Beatrice's ascent to a celestial Jerusalem. Bizarrely, Dante was suddenly a widower to a woman who had never been his wife. He moped round Florence in a dumb and shivering state, gaunt, unshaven, suicidal. Not an hour passed without more wailing and sighs from the lovesick Dante. He seemed to be flying from life. Dante's fellow *stilnovist* poets, among them Cavalcanti, complained that enough was enough: all these moaning griefs were unnatural; worse, they were vulgar. It was no good. The merest glance of sympathy set Dante weeping again. Boccaccio wrote: 'His eyes were like two copious fountains of welling water, so much so that people marvelled where he got enough moisture.' Then one day Dante caught sight of a woman – the famous *donna gentile* (noble lady) – looking at him from a window. Her eyes seemed to regard Dante with compassion and pity ('*pietade*' is the word Dante uses). Was she beckoning him to fall in love? Here was a powerful lure away from his unhappiness. Dante's heart quailed at the prospect. Sentimental Victorian scholars like to imagine that the Lady at the Window might have been Gemma, but could she ever replace Beatrice? Dante wrote sonnets to her, but then reproached himself with infidelity to the memory of Beatrice. He received a *canzone* of sympathy from his poet friend Cino da Pistoia (the narrator of Ezra Pound's dramatic monologue 'Cino'). Cino explains patiently to Dante that life is a serious condition that ultimately proves fatal:

> We know for certain that in this blind world
> Each man's subsistence is grief and pain
> But be comforted: Beatrice has gone to a higher blessedness.
> Look thou into the pleasures wherein dwells
> Thy lovely lady who is in Heaven crown'd,
> Who is herself thy hope in Heaven…

'On the Death of Beatrice Portinari' (translated there by Rossetti into the quasi-Elizabethan idiom so popular in mid-Victorian England) may have helped to bring Dante's grieving to an end. The affair with the mystery woman at the window – most likely she was not Gemma – would be transfigured into the more dazzling love of *The Divine Comedy*. Dante's beloved Beatrice will outlive age and death. She will breathe one breath with Dante. But if, as seems likely, Dante had been married to Gemma Donati for a good seven years, it must have been irksome for her to have a husband continually lachrymose and pining for another woman.

'Here Begins
the New Life'

The *Vita nuova*, born of Dante's friendship with Cavalcanti, is a treatise written by a poet on the art of poetry, and a religious allegory. On Cavalcanti's advice Dante wrote his 'little book' in Florentine vernacular. It combines thirty-one of Dante's early love poems from 1283–92, and tells a story – in prose – of how these sonnets and *canzoni* (as well as one *ballata* or ballad) came into being. The book, one of the strangest vernacular works of the late Middle Ages, is brocaded with enigmas, hallucinatory dream-visions and arcane number symbols. Dante broke new ground with every one of his works and the *Vita nuova*, a landmark in divine self-biography, was no exception. Perhaps it is the 'book of poems' by the thirteenth-century 'Italian poet' to which Bob Dylan alludes in his 1974 song, 'Tangled Up In Blue'.

Beatrice has been dead for three years when the narrative opens in 1293; Dante's father had died ten years earlier. Dante reconfigures and reimagines the past as he tries to make sense of the meaning of human loss. The book's shape had clarified in his mind soon after Beatrice died: it was to be a 'prosimetrum' or a hybrid of prose and poetry such as the medieval philosopher Boethius had popularized in his Latin work, *The Consolation of Philosophy*, which Dante had read as solace in his bereavement. As a spiritual memoir, the *Vita nuova* is indebted too to the fourth-century *Confessions* of St Augustine: like Augustine, Dante is trying to find his way out of a 'dark wood' of past errors, as he revises his past.

For the first time in Western literature, a book offers a collection of poems selected and commented on by the author. The *Vita nuova* is strangely impersonal, for all that, and devoid of descriptive detail or sense of place. Florence is never mentioned, though a Guelf-driven banking boom was about to transform the Tuscan capital from a medieval city on the banks of the Arno into a dynamo that generated untold financial wealth and, soon enough, a splendid mercantile patronage of the arts.

Portrait of Dante from Luca Signorelli's great fresco in the cathedral of
Santa Maria Assunta, Orvieto, Italy, completed between 1499 and 1504 at
the height of the Italian Renaissance.

It is fair to say that no one has taken the *Vita nuova* so seriously as Dante, who intrudes a pedantic and at times wearisomely self-satisfied prose commentary on his own poems. 'This sonnet can be divided into two parts: in the first part I speak of Love as in potentiality; in the second I speak of Love as having passed from potentiality into act.' Boccaccio found the tone of earnest, solemn self-justification 'unnecessary and boring', and he was not alone. Italo Svevo, the great Triestino author (and student of James Joyce), parodied the tone in his 1923 novel, *Zeno's Conscience,* where a Triestine businessman tries in vain to kick a smoking habit. (Zeno's ever-deferred resolution to stop buying cigarettes is couched in terms of a hoped-for religious conversion.)

Mostly, the poems conform to troubadour themes of unrequited love and the obligation to keep secret the identity of the loved one. Dante's intolerable ecstasy in the presence of Beatrice and his anguished mortification at her mockery connects the *Vita nuova* to the poetry of the Sicilian school and the drama of love as Cavalcanti conceived it. Even the lexicon is Cavalcantian: *sbigottito* (bewildered), *orranza* (horror), *struggere* (destroy). As the book progresses, however, Dante questions the nature of possessive desire. If love is not self-interested, what is it? Roland Barthes would ask the same question in *A Lover's Discourse.* The language we use when we are in love is not a language we speak, said Barthes, for it is addressed to ourselves and to our imaginary beloved: it is a language of solitude, a language of mythology. In Beatrice Dante had glimpsed the imprint of divine love. Beatrice's sainted aura serves to contradict, even disqualify Cavalcanti's disillusioning view of love as a delirium and a bitterness, which has now become rather too narrow for Dante's ambition. What Dante was aiming for was a type of 'praise style' (*stilo de la loda*) to justify the title *Vita nuova* with its promise of a life renewed by love. Accordingly, the book records a journey away from the influence of the Sicilian dialect verse of da Lentini, d'Alcamo and d'Aquino to the discovery of a new type of ecstatic, laudatory verse, where the Cavalcantian ideal of painful love has little place.

By the book's end, wonderfully, Beatrice has come to represent an essence beyond her earthly self. She is a paradisiacal being, an ideal of virtue, for whom the very saints in heaven clamour. In a clear rebuttal of Cavalcanti, Dante states that his love was governed always by 'the counsel of reason', not by irrational or negative forces. His new poetry will appeal, Dante hopes, to everyone, not just a select knightly audience of 'gentle hearts' and connoisseurs; *The Divine Comedy* would be made for just such an audience.

In one of the great moments of early Italian prose, Dante describes Beatrice's miraculous effect on him:

> I had no more enemies; instead, I was overcome by a flame of charity which made me forgive all who had offended me; and if anyone had asked me anything at all, my only reply would have been simply, 'Love'...It is therefore obvious that my blessedness lay in her greeting, which often overwhelmed my powers.

The impression of serenity and joy, absent from Dante's earlier panegyrics to his 'sweet lady', derives from what one might call 'the gospel of Beatrice'. Dante has become an evangelist for Beatrice, calling on witnesses to confirm the truth of what he says and spreading knowledge of her God-given transformative power. His celebrated sonnet *Tanto gentile e tanto onesta pare* ('My lady looks so gentle and so pure'), quoted at the book's midway point, stresses the universality of Beatrice's influence. Love, once the cause of so much painful tumult, swoon and shudder, has become a source of sweetness. The sonnet, written in 1290, describes Beatrice at the height of her glory as she walks 'so pleasant in the eyes of men' through the streets of Florence. The Brazilian poet Vinicius de Moraes surely had Beatrice in mind when he wrote the lyrics to the bossa nova anthem 'The

Girl from Ipanema' which, with its languid jazz tones and hushed intensity of emotion, is suffused with a Dantescan yearning for an unnamed but distinctly Beatrician woman:

> Tall and tan and young and lovely
> The girl from Ipanema goes walking
> And when she passes
> Each one she passes goes 'Ah!'

The *Vita nuova* offers a bizarre elaboration on the role played in Beatrice's life by the number nine. Dante was nine years old when he first met Beatrice; nine years had elapsed before she first greeted him. Number nine, a squaring of three, is symbolic of the Holy Trinity; Dante is insistent that Beatrice participate in the *mirabile* ('wondrous') 'three-ness' represented by the Father, the Son and the Holy Ghost. The analogy Dante draws between Beatrice and the Trinity was potentially scandalous as it glorified a mortal woman as the incarnation of transcendence and the Redeemed Life. Three centuries later, in preparation for an ecclesiastical edition of 1576, the Catholic church subjected the *Vita nuova* to censorship. All semi-theological words were removed: *beatitudine* was replaced with the anodyne *felicità* (happiness), while analogies between Christ and Beatrice were excised. Dante was not blasphemous in terms of medieval analogy, however. As a devout Catholic he was permitted to see Beatrice as a 'reflection' of Christ or *speculum Christi* (mirror of Christ); if God had created humanity in his own image, men and women could act as mirrors by 'reflecting' his ways. The justification was lost on the sixteenth-century church inquisitors, however, who initiated an ecclesiastical backlash against Dante that continued right up to the late 1800s.

In many ways, the *Vita nuova* is a dress rehearsal for *The Divine Comedy*. Beneath the book's prose-to-verse retrospection is the story of one man's self-discovery and 'confessional' in the

Catholic sacramental sense of being made anew. The book opens with the Latin words *'Incipit vita nova'* ('Here begins the new life'), and ends with the promise of another book to come. 'I shall write of her what has never been written of any woman.' Whether Dante intended by this *The Divine Comedy* is uncertain but one thing is clear: the work of Beatrice is not yet finished. Only at the close of *Paradiso*, written a quarter of a century later, will Dante's gaze be directed away from his love and towards the ultimate beatific vision. His love for Beatrice will outlive men's lives and the lives of nations, an unsurrendering eternal love.

*

The *Vita nuova* was no sooner finished than Florence became a giant construction site, crisscrossed with scaffolding and teeming with workmen, building materials, towers ruined or lopped off. Dante did not like what he saw. New money was pouring in. The change is attributed to an influx of 'non-Florentine' refugees and migrant workers from neighbouring city-states and especially from the *contado* (countryside), who swelled the city's population from about 30,000 in 1200 to something like 100,000 in 1300. What Dante calls an 'intermingling of peoples' (*confusion de la persone*) is seen as a curse and a cause of discord. Women had taken to wearing gowns cut low to reveal their bosom; their hair was dyed blonde or auburn. The 'purity' of the Florentine blood line was being diluted. And outsiders were to blame. By today's standards, Dante's attitude is dubious, yet his fierce civic pride was not at all unusual for the age. Something of the flavour of his disdain for the *gente nova* (newcomers) would carry over 700 years into the pronouncements made by the model for Anthony Blanche in *Brideshead Revisited*, Sir Harold Acton, the aesthete-dandy who lived for most of his life in a villa outside Florence. In 1985 Sir Harold bewailed the atmosphere of 'weekend Surrey' that had descended on the foreign-dominated (mostly middle-class English) countryside round the Tuscan capital. Florence always had had a strong English connection: *une ville toute anglais*, the Goncourt brothers found Florence in 1855. To Sir Harold's disapproval, Twining's Tea and jars of Marmite were increasingly to be found in Florence. English dabblers of every kind were falling in love with the city; they hoped to bask in the creative aura of Mr and Mrs Robert Browning, but produced only mediocre poems and watercolours. The wreck of Florence was simply too ghastly and heartbreaking for anyone who remembered the old days. New money had poured in to give birth to the monster Sir Harold was pleased to call Chiantishire.

The growing prosperity of Florence in Dante's time as a banking centre and workshop for luxury goods was due entirely to the entrepreneurial industriousness of the Greater and Lesser Guilds. Florence had invented double-entry bookkeeping. Florence was one of the first European cities to pave its streets. In October 1295, the Franciscans began construction of Santa Croce church; a year later, the small Santa Reparata cathedral was transformed into the Santa Maria del Fiore so admired by tourists today. Yet Dante resolutely denounced almost everything that would make Florence great. In February 1299 work commenced on the Palazzo dei Priori (later known as Palazzo della Signoria). By 1300 Florence would have a municipal sewerage system. These projects would take years, sometimes even centuries to complete. The Florence that emerged – the glittering birthplace of the Renaissance – is, largely, the Florence of travel brochures. Chemicals may seep noxiously into the River Arno and Coke cans litter the streets, but one can still imagine the days when Victorian sightseers toured the Uffizi with copies of Ruskin and Walter Pater. Much of the homoerotic art patronized by the Medici banking family would have startled Dante. Michelangelo's *David* (which took just eighteen months to complete) was given proudly blatant genitalia and musculature. In his sonnets, Michelangelo yearned to emulate the melancholic genius of his Florentine master Dante. Donatello's earlier statue of the biblical David – the first life-sized free-standing bronze statue to be created since the classical era – also revels in the boy's naked beauty. Nothing like these statues existed in Dante's Florence; much of that medieval city would be occluded and lost to the Renaissance building programme.

Political Disgrace

Most readers will have some idea of what Dante now looked like. Giovanni Boccaccio described a grave-looking man of 'middle height', who, in later years, grew a beard:

> His face was long, his nose aquiline, and his eyes large rather than small; his jaws big, and his under lip protruding beyond the upper. His complexion was dark, his hair and beard thick, black and curling, and his expression was always melancholy and thoughtful.

The description is not entirely to be trusted: Boccaccio was an unreserved admirer of Dante, whose biography amounts at times to hagiography. Boccaccio never met Dante (he was eight years old when Dante died in 1321). Yet the features he sketched in – the long face, the sharp nose, the jutting jaw – appear in almost all later portraits. From where did Boccaccio's image derive?

A supposed portrait of Dante in the Florentine chapel of the Palazzo del Podestà or Bargello (possibly the work of Giotto) shows a sensitive oval face, beardless, with a straight nose and prognathous chin. Boccaccio was certainly able to see the portrait on the Bargello wall (damaged and poorly restored in 1841). Unfortunately there is no documentary evidence that it is an image of Dante. There are hints enough in the portrait that the scene, the colour, the features do all suggest the poet; but only hints. Dante's prickly personality offers us more certain detail.

The chronicler Giovanni Villani, ten years Dante's junior, drew a rather caustic profile in his 1321 history of Florence. Dante took unreasonable 'delight' in 'grumbling and complaining' about his political exile, says Villani. And he adopted an air of condescending regality – 'presumptuous, contemptuous' – in talking to those he reckoned his intellectual inferiors. Often ill-tempered, Dante was liable to waver between excessive piety and excessively vindictive fury. Boccaccio was careful to agree with Villani on certain of his points. Dante could indeed turn 'furious' when the subject of his exile was raised; however, Boccaccio is ashamed to reveal an impetuous side to Dante: the mad outbursts were undignified. It is clear from the evidence we have that tolerance was not one of Dante's strengths.

Dante never was a Ghibelline, but he developed vehement anti-Guelf sentiments that might at times be mistaken for those of a 'proud Ghibelline', said Boccaccio. The story of how Dante fell out of favour with his fellow Guelfs – the betrayals and back-stabbings, the abuse of power, bribery and partial justice that led to his exile – is Byzantine in its complexity. The immediate cause of Dante's political downfall is not far to seek. Dante was thirty years old when, in 1293, the Florentine government decreed that noble oligarchic families – the so-called *grandi* – were to be excluded from office. The rising middle class of merchants and artisans to which Dante belonged took this as an opportunity to enjoy greater power over the *grandi*. Increasingly the old, land-holding nobility were seen as a hindrance in the new market economy created in Florence by the money-making *popolani*. One result of the political change was to set Guido Cavalcanti implacably against Dante Alighieri: Cavalcanti was a member of one of the seventy or so noble Florentine families banned from political activity.

Like Cavalcanti, Dante's family were Guelfs. As a Guelf city, Florence was in theory allied to the wily Pope Boniface VIII, but allegiances had begun to divide, and dangerously. Though the Guelfs had held power in Florence for a quarter of a century, their division into opposing White and Black factions had resulted in bouts of violence and bloodshed within the city. The Black Guelf leader, Corso Donati, known as *il Barone* (the Baron) for his aggressive political ambition, was the brother of Dante's poet friend Forese Donati (who appears among the 'gluttons' of *Purgatorio*) as well as a cousin of his wife, Gemma Donati. Even though Dante was related to the Blacks by his marriage, he found himself opposed to Donati because his sympathies were

Portrait of a young crimson-robed Dante from a fresco in the Palazzo del Bargello, Florence. The portrait is thought to be by Giotto; to Dante's left, hands in prayer, is his teacher Brunetto Latini.

with the Whites. The antagonism cut deep. Donati's family had recently come into wealth and prominence: they could boast no illustrious ancestry, but were part of the '*gente nuova*' who had caused the degeneration of Florence through what Dante called their 'quick gains' ('*sùbiti guadagni*'). The Blacks were allied to Pope Boniface VIII and set against the merchant class, while the Whites, led by Donati's sworn enemy Vieri de' Cerchi, were now more than ever wary of papal territorial and political ambitions. De' Cerchi, doggedly opposed to all the regulations against the *grandi,* remained aloof from the *popolo,* as Dante was not.

Though Cavalcanti was disbarred from government, he initially supported the Whites, not least because he bitterly detested Corso Donati of the Blacks. Donati had tried to have Cavalcanti killed while he was on pilgrimage in Spain; in retaliation, once he was back home in Florence, Cavalcanti threw a spear at Donati – and missed. Boccaccio's 'rich and graceful knight' Cavalcanti, renowned for his immaculately crafted aristocratic sonnets, had descended to the level of a thug. Factional tensions ran high.

On May Day 1300, violent brawls broke out in Florence as the *grandi* tried to abolish the legislation that penalized them. A man's nose was cut off in the fray. Concerned, Boniface VIII sent a cardinal to Florence in order to make peace but, in spite of his grand-sounding Latin title *paciarius* (peace-maker), he failed, chiefly because Dante and others among the Cerchi-dominated Whites had thwarted his efforts to bring Florence to heel. Dante and his fellow White Guelfs did not approve of the pope throwing his temporal weight about in the republic.

That summer, Dante was elected one of the city's six priors. He held office from 15 June to 14 August 1300 – the year in which the vision of *The Divine Comedy* is set. As all priors were required to be a Greater Guild member, Dante had joined the Guild of Physicians and Apothecaries, who accepted poets. The priorate was the highest office in the Florentine republic, but it brought

Dante only trouble. The cause and origin of all his later hardships came, he later wrote, from 'my unfortunate appointment as prior'. On 23 June, the Eve of the Feast of St John, a group of guild members was again set upon by *grandi*. The priors, hoping to restore order, decided to expel all suspect trouble-makers, White and Black. The Blacks were confined to a castle in Umbria; the Whites, banished to the swampy region of Sarzana in the Lunigiana. Dante's dearest friend Cavalcanti was among the exiled Whites.

In the Sarzana marshlands Cavalcanti fell ill ('how fast life ebbs away'). He was housed in not much more than a thatched hut, stretched out, stricken with the dreaded Genghis ague, today known as malaria. The head-splitting fevers were followed by profuse sweats, his bed a sodden tropical bog. Cavalcanti's great exilic song, '*Perch'i'no spero di tornar giammai*' ('Because No Hope is Left Me To Go Back'), written perhaps from Sarzana, speaks of his 'overwhelming grief' and 'growing fear' at never returning home to Tuscany. He died in August 1300 just a few months after he was in fact recalled to Florence. Dante had personally signed Cavalcanti's exile warrant, which resulted in his death. It was a tragic end to a friendship that had been so important to Dante in his early years. Rarely has the metaphor of the pupil who kills his master been so apt. Cavalcanti would return to haunt Dante in the *Inferno* through the depleted and melancholy figure of his damned father, Cavalcante de' Cavalcanti. Dante had chosen 'justice' over friendship and now his *primo amico* was dead.

It was Dante's misfortune that his new-found political power should coincide with the pope's territorial machinations. Benedetto Caetani had been elected pope with the name Boniface VIII in 1294, having served as rector of St Lawrence's church in Towcester, Northamptonshire. His belief was that 'every human creature should be subject to the Roman pontiff'; only then would man be fit for 'salvation'. His deep-held conviction that the papacy alone could offer universal guidance elevated Boniface above kings and kingdoms, and made him the last great medieval pope. Religious convictions lived side by side in Boniface VIII with worldly ambitions. Hoping to bring Tuscany to heel he set out to exploit tensions between Black and White Guelfs to his own ends. Naturally he supported the pro-papist Black Guelf faction under the hoodlum Donati. The White Guelfs, feeling threatened, accused Boniface of simony – the trafficking of ecclesiastical preferment for money. The accusation was not unfounded. The pope had offered a 'full and copious pardon' to all pilgrims who visited Rome during the Holy Jubilee Year of 1300 (the year that Dante was made prior). The mass plenary absolution caught the imagination of Europe, and, it was said, enriched Roman churches to such an extent that sacristans had to scoop in offerings with rakes.

Over 200,000 penitents – twice the number of the Florentine population – made for the basilica of St Peter. Canto 18 of the *Inferno* compares a double file of naked sinners ('pimps' and 'seducers') swarming past each other in opposite directions to the crowds in Rome as they submit to the pope's police control on Ponte Sant'Angelo; those going to St Peter's (and facing the Castel Sant'Angelo) had to keep to one side of the Tiber bridge; those leaving St Peter's (facing Monte Giordano – 'the mount') to the other. The sinners, whipped along by horned devils, keep up a steady two-way traffic:

> Just as the Romans dealt with the pilgrims
> this Jubilee year, over the bridge,
> handling the flow of people,
>   so on one side they all headed
> to the Castle, going to St Peter's,
> and on the other they moved as one to the mount.

The description has the flavour of eye-witness reportage.

Dante's attitude to Rome as the seat of the papacy was not yet scornful; quite the contrary: he was awed by the 'noble city, of which the very stones of the encircling walls are worthy of reverence'. The babble of the pilgrims' many foreign tongues provided Dante with his first awareness of the variety and dimensions of a Europe beyond Florence, a Europe of strange tongues. It is no coincidence that Dante chose to set the allegory of his own life-pilgrimage, *The Divine Comedy,* in Easter Week of that Jubilee year of 1300: it is thought that Dante was himself among the thousands who took part in the church's Jubilee.

Politics were set to ensnare and bring Dante down. The White–Black Guelf turmoil was of very grave concern to Boniface, who coveted Florence as a financial powerhouse. Having (rightly) suspected the White Guelfs of anti-papal ambitions he consolidated his support for the Blacks. This he did by appointing Charles of Valois, brother of King Philip IV of France, as an intermediary, though his secret remit was to conquer Florence for the church. Unsurprisingly the Whites did not trust Charles: both he and the pope (they believed, rightly) had no respect for Florentine independence. Like Siena, Pisa, Lucca, Arezzo, Pistoia and the other central Italian city-states, Florence remained autonomous and self-governing. Its survival as an independent commune (republic) was under threat.

In October 1301 Corso Donati of the Black Guelfs called on Charles in nearby Siena. As well as a promise of papal favours he offered a sum of 70,000 florins (almost £8,000,000 in today's terms) in support of his 'peace-keeping' mission in Florence. The Whites, anxious to gain assurances from the pope that Charles would uphold the Florentine constitution, hurriedly sent three representatives to Rome. Dante, dressed in his prior's ermine-trimmed crimson robes, was part of the three-man embassy whose task was to plead with the pope to call off his emissary, Charles de Valois.

Dante's detested Pope Boniface VIII, from a fresco by Giotto in the Basilica of St John Lateran, Rome.

Unsurprisingly the Pope received the triumvirate coldly. Boniface had made up his mind, and had no intention of changing it. Two of the delegation were dismissed but Dante was detained in Rome in the hope, it seems, of involving him in a bargaining compact or concession. Charles of Valois arrived at the gates of Florence on 1 November, All Saints' Day. He was accompanied by 200 Tuscan knights, who, apparently, had come to honour the king of France's brother, lodged now in quarters across the River Arno. The priors had no choice but to hand over control of Florence. Charles, reassuringly, swore to keep the peace. Three days later, however, Corso Donati arrived accompanied by an army of fellow exiled Blacks, all of them armed. Charles did nothing to impose restraint; on the contrary, Dante said later, he carried only the 'lance' of 'Judas', in other words, of betrayal. Black Guelf supporters, having been released from jail, set about pillaging and murdering Whites.

By 8 November all the White Guelf priors, Dante included, had been ousted and replaced by Black Guelfs. Dante was probably still in Rome at the time of the November coup; he arrived in Siena soon after, where he heard that the situation in Florence was forlorn. Dante never forgave Pope Boniface VIII for his part in Florence's downfall. Of all the evil-doers in *The Divine Comedy*, the pope is the most repeatedly reviled and execrated. The Blacks, having set the judicial machinery in motion, began to sentence Whites to banishment. The trials of 27 January condemned Dante for a crime he probably did not commit. This was *baractaria*, barratry, making illicit profit from public office (*lucra illecita et inquinas extorsiones*) – a medieval form of sleaze. Dante was, however, guilty of two other crimes. These were promoting the expulsion from nearby Pistoia of the Black Guelfs, and refusal to supply military assistance to the pope. Failure to answer charges at a trial was tantamount to a confession of guilt: Dante was sentenced to imprisonment and fined 5,000 florins payable within three days. He failed to show up at the sentencing. On 10 March 1302, six weeks later, the investigators declared that Dante would burn to death at the stake (*igne comburatur sic quod moriatur*) should he ever return to Florence. By the end of that year, no fewer than 559 death sentences had been passed. The names of the condemned were recorded in a parchment codex, *Il libro del chiodo* (The Book of the Nails), so-called because of the menacing large nails impressed on the leather-covered boards, front and back. Dante Alighieri's name is legible among those of the other 'Rebel Families of the City of Florence'. Curious recurring symbols at the tops of the pages – a horse's head, a billy goat, a castle – represent the various *sestieri* or quarters of Florence. They represent also an atrocious display of human intolerance.

Banished from Florence, Dante was unable to reach out to his wife. But since Gemma was of the Donati dynasty and a cousin of the Black Guelf leader Corso Donati, Dante could at least be sure that she and the children were safe. This seems to have been the case. But there was no future now for Dante in politics, or in Florence: the Blacks mocked and jeered at the lost White souls and their fallen hopes.

Exile

Dante never went back to Florence. The murderous Black Guelf violence there and destruction of White Guelf properties made return impossible. Under sentence of death the poet-politician could have been killed legitimately, and with impunity, by anyone in Florence at any time. According to Boccaccio, Dante was forced to flee into exile alone, 'leaving behind his wife, together with the rest of his family'. Under cover of dark, relatives hid his possessions for safekeeping in a Franciscan monastery (what possessions, Boccaccio does not say). Gemma apparently remained in Florence, her marriage effectively at an end. She would have been ill-advised to follow her husband into exile immediately, as he had yet to find financial resources or patrons. Gemma's oldest two sons, Pietro and Jacopo, would themselves have to endure banishment once they reached the age of fourteen.

Much of what happened in Dante's exile remains obscure, especially the early years. In all probability he stayed in central and northern Italy; stories of visits to southern France, or studies in Paris or even Oxford, are very likely fabrications. Dante was most likely on his own, though scholars have argued that he was accompanied for some of the time by Pietro and Jacopo (who were among the first to write commentaries on *The Divine Comedy*), as well as by his daughter, who became a nun and took 'Beatrice' as her name in religion. We cannot know for sure.

Driven from home ('guiltlessly exiled', Dante said), the thirty-seven-year-old former prior wished devoutly to return to Florence and sometimes he must have wondered emotionally if he had ever left. Banishment came as a disaster to one who believed, as Dante firmly did, that an individual's good was bound up with the good of his society, for his most immediate and cherished society was that of Florence. Life hardened obdurately against Dante as he began to wander from patron to patron, from place to place up and down the northern part of the Italian peninsula in search of employment, either as a diplomat or court official; proving, in his own bitter words, 'How hard going up and down another man's stairs is',* *come è duro calle lo scendere e 'l salir per l'altrui scale'* (canto 17 of *Paradiso*).

So unhappy was Dante during his first years of banishment that he consorted even with the enemy Ghibellines. Reduced almost to beggary, he was often hungry as he traipsed companionless across the Apennine mountains to the foothills of Romagna. Shame – the shame of poverty, the shame of exile – now dominated his life. His letters from this time were signed: 'Dante Alighieri, Florentine, exile undeservedly'. What hurt Dante most was not the poverty, homelessness or loss of social status, but the 'infamy' of his conviction, which had left his character permanently defamed. He walked everywhere with a sense of his own criminality. In a poem from this time Dante condemns Florence as a pitiless city 'devoid of love' (*vota d'amore*); typically he addresses the poem as if it were a human being capable of independent life:

> Oh mountain song, you can go:
> Perhaps you'll see Florence, my home,
> That has locked me out,
> Loveless and devoid of love.

From exile, Dante watched the gradual weakening of his nemesis Corso Donati's influence and his final ruin. Donati had only six years left to live. In 1308, accused of conspiring with Ghibellines to overthrow the Florentine republic, he was murdered in Florence by his own former allies. Dante, in *Purgatorio*, imagines Donati caught in his horse's stirrup and dragged in a race towards Hell. (Corso's sister, Picarda Donati, bizarrely, is found among the blessed of *Paradiso*.) Though exile was a time of despair and 'painful' poverty for Dante, it brought a

---

* See verse p. 136.

overleaf
Dante in laurels (to signify his greatness) from a 1509–10 fresco by the Renaissance artist Raphael. The gold-dressed pope to the left is Sixtus IV.

purifying clarity to his literary vision. For one thing, it freed him from too narrow a pride in his native Tuscany. Italians call loyalty to one's hometown *campanilismo* (from *campanile,* 'bell tower'). In lands far distant from the metaphoric 'bell tower' of Florence, Dante discovered peoples, food and, most important, dialects different from his own. He came to realize that the Italian language was more fragmented and various than he had ever imagined. 'The people of Padua speak one way', he marvelled, 'and those of Pisa another.' More extraordinary still, speech differed even among those 'who live in the *same* city, such as the Bolognese who live in Borgo San Felice and the Bolognese who live in Strada Maggiore.' How had these medieval vernaculars come into being? Throughout his seven exile years from 1302–9 Dante identified a total of fourteen different dialects. The Florentine who had scarcely ventured outside his native city found unexpected horizons opening up before him. While Tuscan would inevitably predominate over other dialects in *The Divine Comedy*, the poem would contain traces of Neapolitan, Lombard, Arabic, Sardinian, as well as Pisan-Lucchese, Siculo-Tuscan, ancient Greek, Latin and Hebrew. Dante, Italy's first known dialectologist, anticipated much modern linguistics in his intuition that languages themselves change and have histories. Without his wandering days in exile, Dante would not have understood as much.

The politics of Dante's wavering White–Black loyalties are less easy to fathom. In June 1302 he met a group of White Guelfs exiled to the Mugello region north of Florence; later, in the autumn, he followed Whites across the Apennines to Forlì – the centre of the Romagnole Ghibellines who had allied themselves, opportunistically, to the Whites. The following year, 1303, he stayed for ten months in Verona at the pro-Ghibelline court of Bartolomeo della Scala, where he found other Florentine exiles, among them members of the Alighieri family, cousins on his father's side.

On 15 February, in Verona, Dante watched the Lenten horse races, where the winner was traditionally awarded a length of green cloth. The races would find their way into the *Inferno*: Dante's old teacher Brunetto Latini is seen to run off naked over the burning sands like one of those Verona athletes who 'competes for the green cloth'. Situated on the Adige river in the Veneto, Verona had one of the richest libraries in all Europe, the Biblioteca Capitolare or Chapter Library. No castle or other retreat in the Tuscan or Romagnan Apennines had a library sufficiently stocked to satisfy Dante's intellectual curiosities. Among the Chapter Library's collection dating back to the fifth and sixth centuries were Greek manuscripts illustrating the life of Christ, the purple-dyed vellum pages gleaming gold with whorls of Byzantine interlace. In the library's atmosphere of reverence and awe, Dante conceived the idea of *De vulgari eloquentia,* the first serious attempt to articulate the idea of a national vernacular language. Begun in about 1304, his brief study of Italian alludes to such Latin writers as Pliny (whether the Elder or the Younger is unclear), Livy and Frontinus, who were scarcely known at that time on the Italian peninsula, but who were catalogued at the Biblioteca Capitolare.

On 12 October 1303, while Dante was in Verona, Pope Boniface VIII died after supporters of Philip IV of France physically assaulted him at his home in Anagni. No love was lost between Philip and the pope, not least because the French king levied taxes on the clergy without papal consent. Christian Europe was nevertheless shocked by the death. The new pope, Benedict XI, preached that Christ himself had been assailed in the person of His own vicar on earth: the pope. Strange to say, given his later antipathy to Boniface, Dante agreed with Benedict. In canto 20 of *Purgatorio*, Philip IV is maligned as 'the new Pilate', who washed his hands of responsibility for the sacrilegious assault.

Almost certainly Dante afterwards went to Arezzo, the White

Guelf headquarters, but there he quarrelled so fiercely with fellow exiles that he broke away from the Whites to form, as he said, 'a party of himself alone'. Bologna, seventy miles from Florence, was where Dante stayed next. The sight of the city's russet and pink-toned buildings provided a measure of consolation. For two years from July 1304 to early 1306 Dante was pleasurably detained at the great city of Emilia-Romagna. With its geometric Roman street plan and fantastic leaning towers, Bologna was (still is) the undisputed culinary heart of Italy; nowhere (according to the Bolognese) was the pasta so rich and creamy, or the meat such a bright, sanguinous red. Many of Bologna's lewd medieval street names (Via Fregatette – 'Rub-Tits Street') date from Dante's time. Dante ate well and, most important, renewed his friendship with the Tuscan vernacular poet Cino da Pistoia, who taught jurisprudence at Bologna university, one of the oldest in Europe. Dante had known Cino since Beatrice died in 1290, sixteen years earlier, and Cino had sent him a *canzone* of condolence. It made no difference to Dante that Cino was a Black Guelf as a part of him hungered for release from Black–White conformities. Just as the *Vita nuova* claimed Guido Cavalcanti as its guiding light, so *De vulgari* would claim Cino da Pistoia as its inspiration. The musicality and rhetorical skill of Cino's verse, admired by, among others, Petrarch, was ranked with the very highest by a select few in Bologna. In *De vulgari* Dante exalts Cino (a touch cravenly) as Italy's foremost love poet.

Strikingly analytical and reflective, *De vulgari* considers the origin and history of language from its fragmentation following the biblical Tower of Babel to the medieval present. Written on the eve of *The Divine Comedy*'s birth, the book is self-consciously provisional in design, and indeed remains unfinished. In fourteen brief chapters, Dante maps out the terrain of the vernacular on the Italian peninsula, and emerges as a trenchant, even a militant critic as he does so. 'Since we do not find that anyone before us has treated of the science of the Vulgar Tongue', he announces, 'we will endeavour, by the aid of the Wisdom which breathes from Heaven, to be of service to the speech of the common people.'

It might seem odd that a treatise in defence of the vernacular was written in Latin, what Dante elsewhere calls a *lingua artificialis*. Yet Dante knew that his book would find a greater readership among scholars and philosophers in Latin, because Latin remained the bedrock of the medieval educational system and the language of authority. It is a shame that *De vulgari* has been relegated to Dante's *opere minori* ('minor works') because of the shadow cast over them by *The Divine Comedy*. It is the greatest hymn of praise ever written in honour of the Italian language. Nowhere does Dante claim that Italian is superior to Latin, or vice versa. His other great 'minor work' of this period, *Convivio* (The Banquet), a philosophical study of the intellectual and theological concerns of the age, exalts Latin, not the vernacular, as the higher medium. The grammatical precision and unchanging ('incorruptible') nature of Latin is evident in Virgil's *Aeneid*, which Dante upholds as a picturesque and vigorous pre-Christian marvel. At the same time, confusingly, *De vulgari* calls for a reformed vernacular that would eventually supersede the 'inefficacious' and 'ill-conceived' Latin. For all his inconsistencies, Dante is unwavering in his determination to raise the cultural stock of the *volgare*. The poetic greatness that classical authors had displayed though Latin, Dante was determined to display through the vulgar tongue in the work that he was now incubating.

More so than Provençal or French, Italian is the medium best suited to the 'most subtle of poets', says Dante, among them 'Cino da Pistoia and his friend (*amicus ejus*)' – that is, Dante Alighieri. After this deft compliment to his vernacular poet-jurist friend, Dante considers the more egregiously dislikeable (in his view) Italian dialects. Spoleto, Ancona, Milan, Bergamo, Aquileia,

Istria, the Casentino and Prato all have dialects which elicit Dante's contempt for their perceived dissonance and cacophony. Yet they are not the worst offenders. The coarse-tongued language of Rome – 'ugliest of all the Italian dialects' – was rebarbative. No less displeasing to Dante was the Sicilian vulgate, again confusingly so, as he had so admired the Sicilian poets under Frederick II with their languid Eastern hymns in praise of roses. As for Sardinians, they were not even Italian; they spoke Latin 'as apes imitate men'.

Inevitably, an element of national pride informs Dante's elevation of Tuscan. His dream for Tuscan was that it would become a 'grammatical' language that combined the *universalitas* of Latin with the *naturalitas* of biblical Hebrew (the language first spoken by Adam in the Garden of Eden). Tuscan was superior not only to Latin but to all other vernaculars spoken on the peninsula. It was so musical, moreover, that it was almost inherently poetic, and was imbued with the 'natural' nobility of a language spoken 'at our mother's knee' in Florence. Tuscan was, in Dante's formulation, a natural, Edenic language – God's gift to the human race. And, furthermore, it was illuminated by the economic powerhouse that was Florence, so that a 'lustre' was conferred automatically on those who used it. Only a vernacular of such manifest virtues could allow the scattered court intellectuals and scholars of late thirteenth-century Italy to create a poetry of the most noble (Dante calls it 'tragic') kind. It was capable, Tuscan, not only of transcending narrow city loyalties – *campanilismo* – but of being enriched by other forms of Italian and transalpine languages. Once strained of provincial and municipal impurities, Tuscan could take on the God-given properties of a language of grace.

In a real sense, then, Tuscan was to play its part in Dante's salvation: by using a language infused with the utterance of the Holy Spirit, the repentant poet would become a 'signifier of the divine' and we, his readers, would share in his penitent honesty and pray for his rescue. Whether from an inherited flaw of human nature or taint of original sin, Dante certainly saw himself as a fallen man in need of consolation following Beatrice's death. Dante's determination to give Italy a language that would be adequate to the 'highest message' written since the Bible would find expression in *The Divine Comedy*. By 'highest message' Dante meant his own project. In seeking to be true to his loved one to raise up its language and tradition, Dante would be idealized as a forerunner of the national revival movement that became known in nineteenth-century Italy as the Risorgimento.

Convivio, Dante's longest prose work and also unfinished, was aimed at a general readership among the literate and affluent laity, or, as Dante put it, 'princes, barons, knights, and many other noble folk, not just men but women'. The book encouraged Florentines to leave behind any sense of inferiority they might have about Latin, and embrace Tuscan as the *vulgare illustre* (illustrious dialect). Written at the same time as *De vulgari*, the book was supposed to offer fourteen of Dante's own poems to be 'eaten' on trenchers of 'bread' (prose commentary). All this would provide a 'banquet' (*convivio*) of knowledge and philosophy to be enjoyed intellectually. The image of a readership seated at the table of Philosophy, who might benefit from morsels of the banquet that Dante wishes to provide for them, was mirrored in the earthly banquets of Dante's own day. Often such meals were stately, elaborate affairs in which main dishes were carried into the hall in splendour, sometimes balanced on the back of a horse; cooks, caterers, pages, courtiers, footmen and artisans together might help to prepare a giant boiled sturgeon decorated with the host's coat of arms picked out in garlic and red sauce. The imaginary banquet of the *Convivio* was an invitation to all who could read to feast together on a rarefied food for the mind. Only four of the book's projected fourteen chapters were completed. These have much to say about why Dante chose to write in Tuscan instead of the 'philosophically more respectable Latin', and boldly pronounce *toscano* equal to – but not necessarily superior to – Latin for refinement of expression. The book reflects deeply too on the nature of true nobility. What is nobility of birth? What kind of society best fosters it? The 'false and vile' judgment that nobility is based solely on wealth is refuted. Nobility is a property of human nature, not of money. The idea may be commonplace in our egalitarian age: the *Convivio,* though, is the first known articulation of this 'bourgeois' meritocratic idea. Chaucer, in 'The Wife of Bath's Tale' from the Canterbury cycle, cites Dante as an authority for this view of 'gentillesse' (in Italian, *gentilezza*) as a sort of benevolence of spirit. Courtesy is a quality that Beatrice will perceive in the Mantua-born Virgil. '*O anima cortese mantoana*' ('O courteous Mantuan soul'), she addresses him at the beginning of the *Inferno*, at a moment when she herself is on a most courteous errand, the salvation of her lover. Beatrice's own 'gentility of spirit' is innate, untainted by greed or a desire for political preferment. It is intimately connected with love. 'Love', wrote Tyndale, translating St Paul, 'suffereth long and is courteous'.

Dante was in his early forties when he wrote the *Convivio*. The lyric poetry and love stories that inspired the *Vita nuova* fifteen years earlier must have seemed as remote to him now as his lost Florentine homeland. But love, with all its mysteries, has not deserted him. The 'gentle lady' of the *Vita nuova* becomes in the *Convivio* 'Lady Philosophy', and in this guise she shadows and replicates Beatrice as the force that motivates Dante's new quest to shine light on 'the state of souls after death', as he described *The Divine Comedy*'s purpose. Dante's *canzone* from this time, many of them, launch bitter and resentful attacks on meanness, considered the worst of the 'uncourtly' vices, because it kills generosity which, like courtesy, is one of the foundations of noble behaviour. Other pre-*Divine Comedy* poems condemn the abuse of wealth by Florentine parvenus, exhibitionists and prodigals who 'preen' and 'prink' themselves on their material promiscuity and possessions. Young Guelf bankers and young Ghibelline bankers alike had taken to scenting their gloves with ambergris, a sperm-whale secretion; with their obsessive attention to fashion, and frivolity, they were the equivalent of Rolex-wearing, Savile Row-suited bucks about town, and would thus be condemned to aeons of pain in the *Inferno*.

With these two works of his middle period – *De vulgari* and the *Convivio* – Dante the disgraced politician, guilty of barratry and embezzlement, sought to re-establish himself as a scholar and a poet, and to restore his battered self-confidence. The books failed to do that: neither was much circulated at the time. It was only with *The Divine Comedy* that the exile would free himself from infamy and the harsh tumult of his life away from home.

Absolute Hell
(Move over, Lucifer)

The inferno of the living is already here…the inferno where we
live every day, that we form by being together.
ITALO CALVINO, *Invisible Cities*

I myself am Hell,
nobody's here –
ROBERT LOWELL, 'Skunk Hour'

Exactly when Dante began to write the first book of *The
Divine Comedy,* the *Inferno,* is uncertain; most scholars agree
on 1308, six years into the poet's banishment from Florence.
Something extraordinary must have happened to the exile then
– a conversion, an awakening – because he left both the *Convivio*
and *De vulgari* unfinished. And then embarked on a work which
he hoped would bring not only his own salvation but that of
all benighted Christian Europe. How Dante came to write so
outrageously presumptuous a work remains a mystery. Over-
ambitious projects are objectionable in many fields, but perhaps
less so in literature, which is reinvigorated only when writers
dare to attempt the new (the really new). The three-part poem
glowed with such a sharp-edged verismo that contemporaries
suspected a supernatural intervention. The name 'Dante',
Boccaccio speculated, meant 'divine gift' or 'the giver': Dante
had been 'given' the gift of poetry. In writing *The Divine Comedy*
the poet was literally doing God's work; he was *scriba Dei.* On its
completion in 1320, the poem would run to 14,233 lines.

The process of the poem's physical composition is unknown.
Part of the problem is that we know so little about Dante's life
in exile: where he stayed, for how long – almost nothing. In all
likelihood Dante circulated *The Divine Comedy* in batches of
cantos as he completed them: but which cantos? There is no
agreement even on what the cantos looked like on the page, or
with what quill or what pen Dante wrote them. Since he spent
the last ten years of his life in Verona and Ravenna, the first

copyists were likely to have been northern Italian. Or perhaps Dante himself made copies (if so, they are lost). How many copies were made and how many copies Dante could afford to have made, given his circumstances in exile, is also unknown. We do know that the *Inferno* and *Paradiso* were circulated in 1317 and 1319 respectively, and that Dante probably never prepared a complete copy of his poem for publication. This was most likely done in about 1322 in Ravenna by his son Jacopo soon after his father's death. *The Divine Comedy* circulated originally as a codex – a book made by sewing together folded sheets. Whether it was reproduced on paper or parchment is also a mystery. The poem's success seems to have been immediate. Its genius was celebrated in schools, on the street, and, by the end of the 14th century, in the pulpit.

Dante's handwriting was 'thin and long and very accurate', according to Leonardo Bruni, secretary to the Florentine Republic from 1427 to 1444 (Bruni had been able to see letters in the poet's hand). Presumably it was in this semi-formal Gothic script that Dante began composition. *The Divine Comedy* was written in the triple rhyme scheme known as the *terza rima* which Dante invented. The interlaced rhyming tercets lend the poem a tremendous forward momentum and drumbeat stress pattern. Together, the 100 cantos (from the Latin *cantus,* 'song') provided confirmation that the Florentine vernacular could match and even surpass anything that Latin had so far achieved. The poem's carefully structured tripartite design (*L'Inferno*, *Purgatorio*, *Paradiso*), the poetic beauty of the parts and their encyclopedic span and linguistic range: all this was unprecedented. Dante had effectively created his own genre with *The Divine Comedy* and was wholly and admirably himself. As with Homer's *Odyssey* the poem derives from an ancient tradition of poetry as song. ('I sing of arms and the man', the *Aeneid* begins.) Dante makes this clear through numerous addresses in the singular to his reader

('I swear, Reader', 'As you well know'), and occasionally by using *voi*, indicating a plural audience or readership. Just as Virgil 'sang' his verse epic, so Dante's 'comedy' is a 'song' or a poem in the medieval sense of a *'detto'* – precisely, words spoken or sung. The *Inferno* is full of addresses of this sort: only rarely does Dante present the work as words written on a page. Until the invention of printing, *The Divine Comedy* would not, for the most part, have been read but heard. In order to catch the ear, the poem proceeds as in a chant, with a rhythm that approaches music.

Always breaking convention, Dante significantly extended the 'comic' register of medieval literature though his mosaic-like borrowings from classical works and the Bible. The quick repartee of the *piazza* coexists in the poem with the sweet style of the *stilnovo*. Dante is often compared to Milton: each poet was stern and severe in his condemnation of human sin. But Milton has one music only: the literary 'sublime', characterized by a majestic and noble Latinate language that soared. In Dante, by contrast, the music is polyphonic and multilingual; it incorporates elements of *turpiloquium* (lewd talk) and *scurrilitas* (scurrilous joking). In calling his poem a 'comedy' Dante may in fact have intended a humble rhetoric that encompasses a myriad linguistic registers and levels of reality. The nonsense baby talk that opens canto 7 of the *Inferno* – '*Papé Satàn, papé Satàn aleppe!*' – anticipates the lexical innovations of James Joyce ('...there was a moocow coming down along the road...') Umberto Eco, for one, found in Dante a hybrid medieval-modernist, whose proto-Joycean wordplay provided him with the title for his posthumous 2016 essay collection, *Papé Satàn Aleppe*.

One of the more modern aspects of *The Divine Comedy* is that it contains within itself the story of its own making. At the end of *Purgatorio* Beatrice appears before Dante. The moment is intensely personal and dramatic; Virgil, who has been the poet's guide and support until now, has suddenly disappeared. For the first and only time in the poem the author is identified by name. Beatrice addresses him: 'Dante, though Virgil goes away, you must not weep, do not weep yet.' Almost in a theatrical aside, Dante apologizes to the reader for using his own name: his name is registered only out of necessity. What necessity Dante does not say, but at this point everything has turned into writing, as *The Divine Comedy* self-consciously exploits its own literariness. The journey necessitated into the afterlife by Dante's spiritual renewal is bound up self-consciously with the writing of the poem. Such reflexivity foreshadows the concern of contemporary Italian writers such as Italo Calvino, who were often more interested in the adventure of writing stories than in stories that tell of adventures. Of course, there is an inescapable circularity in any conscious reflection on language through the medium of language but in Dante that self-consciousness becomes an occasion for wickedly effective pastiche, philosophic humour, adrenaline-quickening horror, grotesque drollery and, often, a sensuous immediacy of detail. Beneath *The Divine Comedy*'s fearsome erudition was a writer with a vocation for wit and satire. Dante displays a strong weakness for paradox and oxymoron throughout ('barren hope', 'burning cold'), along with a variety of interests ranging from Arabic astronomical and cosmological theory to the chivalric romances of medieval France. Calvino's 1956 collection of minimalist fables concerning the origin of Planet Earth, *Cosmicomics,* owes much to *The Divine Comedy* in the use it makes of the language of astronomy, physics, geometry, optics, medicine, philosophy and cosmogony (literally, 'world-birth').

On one level, then, *The Divine Comedy* offers an apology for a work of literature as a vast network that links all things. In a famous bookbinding image at the end of *Paradiso*, Dante gazes up at the stars and perceives the unity of creation as a volume whose pages are bound together through the operation of divine love:

> In its depth I saw that it contained,
> bound up by love into a single volume,
> all the leaves scattered through the universe.

The scattered 'leaves' here are like the constituent parts of a medieval manuscript. Copied by scribes, the pages could circulate separately or – as in Dante's image – be stitched together to form a single volume. The French symbolist poet Stéphane Mallarmé's bleakly textual notion that nothing of any real significance exists outside language (*'tout aboutit en un livre'* – everything exists in order to 'end up in a book') has points in common with Dante's imagined world as a 'single volume'. Dante believed that the whole universe could be read as if it were the living word of God. Human experience itself might be thought of as learning to read and understand the world around us. *The Divine Comedy* is a work about the universe that contains the multiplicity of all books, but with a maximum concentration of poetry and thought. Immense cosmologies, sagas and epics are reduced in the poem to the dimension of simple exempla.

In Dante, all is symmetry. Hell, shaped like a gigantic inverted funnel, is divided into the Ante-Inferno and nine concentric circles sloping precipitously downward. The first five circles form the Upper Inferno; the last four, the Lower Inferno. Within Hell are crypts, pits, precipices, dunes; at its apex, the place most remote from God, is Lucifer-Satan, 'the worm that gnaws the world'. Purgatory is situated in what today is Australia: the Antipodes. The three supernatural worlds traversed by Dante the pilgrim poet are mapped with pinpoint accuracy. Like a careful workman Dante divided Purgatory into nine 'cornices' (*cornice*), with each cornice representing a different form of suffering. On the first cornice the sinners are weighed down by stones carried on their backs, atoning metaphorically for the 'burden' of pride. In the cornice of envy the sinners have their eyes sewn up: envy was thought to enter through the eyes.

Italo Calvino relaxing at his flat in Paris a year before he died of a cerebral haemorrhage in 1984, at the age of 61.

For all its religious intent, *The Divine Comedy* was potentially an ecclesiastical scandal: not only did it consign six popes to Hell, it denounced the corrupted rites and rituals of the Holy Roman Church, called for the surrender of all the wealth it had accumulated over a millennium and for it to abandon any influence in secular affairs. (Dante was a fierce anti-hierocrat: he did not believe in government by religious leaders.) A part of Dante saw himself as a prophet come among mankind to cauterize the human heart of sin and guide the people of Italy onto the right path. His head at this point was fabulously full of himself.

The *Inferno* opens with Dante-the-pilgrim lost in the Gothic darkness of a wood. It is unclear how long Dante stays in the wood. But the wood is so palpably real – 'savage, harsh and dense' – that the mere memory of it induces '*paura*' (fear) in him. Everything is a pitch dark, static lifelessness; the pilgrim-poet is hardly able to see his hand in front of his face, or put one foot in front of the other. He walks like one who is 'devoid of life' or *fuor di vita*, as Cavalcanti put it in a sonnet. We are in a melancholy place full of menace, with just a faint pre-dawn glow and a glister from the moon. The menace, like that of the 'ruthless, deadful' woods of Shakespeare's *Titus Adronicus*, exemplifies an old idea of fallen nature. Dante has lost himself utterly in these dire woods, with no guarantee that he will ever find himself or else be found. The enveloping darkness suggests not just an ache in Dante's soul and body but his emotional ignorance ('dark', in variants of West Indian English today, means 'stupid' or 'unintelligent'). Dante is so far gone in self-confusion that he has wandered off the '*verace via*' – the righteous way. He is living a life disconnected from human hope and is the saddest man on earth. Aristotle might have spoken of his 'incontinence' – a man unable to order his appetites to his reason: morality, in Aristotle's ethics of moderation, consisted in finding the middle way through reason. With its trees that press menacingly in on Dante and a sense of malign

Dante lost in the dark woods of the opening canto of *The Divine Comedy*. Gustave Doré's illustration radiates a shadowy menace.

spirits lying in wait to do mischief, the wood expresses its poet's inner moral landscape. He is green with fear, vice-ridden and, for the moment, alienated from heavenly grace. Appropriately the wood has no precise topographical location; we are not even told how Dante got there, nor does he seem to know. All the poet knows is that he has strayed grievously. Centuries later, Samuel Beckett's Molloy will confess from within the confines of his dim-lit room: 'I don't know how I got there', adding: 'What I'd like now is to speak of the things that are left, say my goodbyes, finish dying.' So it was with Dante: with *The Divine Comedy* he hoped to set a crown upon all his writing to date, and offer a testimonial of his life before it was too late. At a time of plague or some other calamity in late medieval Europe the life expectancy of a man was thirty; Dante was thirty-five – close to Christ's age at the crucifixion. The dark wood may be taken to reflect the poet's – forgive the anachronism – midlife crisis. He has passed the prime of life. Where now? When now? What now? In the *Vita nuova* Dante had compared himself to one 'who cannot decide what path to take'; a decade on he is still further astray.

The man in the wood is at once Dante Alighieri late of Florence and Everyman, reporting on his own sense of spiritual travail and, eventually, the way forward to man's rescue. He is no hero or man of action: Dante undertakes this journey because superior powers demand it. St Augustine, in his *Confessions*, had likewise represented himself as both a sinner and a vessel of revelation. Dante's eye-witness and ear-witness account of this shadowy place reflects a generalized feeling of foreboding such as E. M. Forster described in his 1903 tale 'The Story of a Panic', where a group of English tourists experience acute anxiety in the chestnut woods above Ravello. A malicious creature – the Greek god Pan – has blown panic into their souls. Dante's spiritual torpor seems to have redoubled in the wood's extinguished daylight, his interior darkness more terrible than the exterior gloom. Up until this moment his life had been a confused immersion in Guelf-Ghibelline feuds, Black–White Guelf hatreds and other secular dead-ends.

> It's no easy thing to talk about,
> this place, so drear and dismal
> I shudder even now to think of it.
> Death itself is hardly more bitter.

As day breaks, the rising sun warms the air, and light suffuses the wood. Dante takes heart when he sees ahead of him a mountaintop radiant in the daybreak; it is not entirely clear which mountain this is, but the canto's dream-like tone suggests Mount Purgatory:

> I looked up: the hilltop
> was robed in the planet's rays
> that guide the traveller on every road.

Dante is about to ascend the hill and, he hopes, escape the wood when a leopard-like animal impedes him. The leopard is a medieval allegory of sensuality or lust, just as the lion and the she-wolf that impede Dante's way soon after are allegories of pride and greed. The three beasts push the poet back further into the wood's wild tracts. Dante's first encounter in *The Divine Comedy* is thus not with human beings: his only human company is his own. Escape seems hopeless yet release does eventually come. Dante's gaze falls on a dim human figure. A shade? An actual man? The figure turns out to be Virgil, the supreme poet of antiquity, but Dante does not know this yet. The apparition is hoarse-voiced because he has been silent for thirteen centuries.

> Someone appeared before my eyes,
> hoarse from long silence, it seemed.
> When I saw him in this great desert

I cried out to him, 'Living man or ghost,
whatever you are, have pity on me'.

The apparition answers that he was born before Christ at a time '*sub Julio*' – when Julius Caesar ruled over Rome. He has been sent by Beatrice in heaven to rescue Dante, and show him a way out of this darkness so that he can understand better why we are here in this world. 'O mighty poet, help me', Dante implores. But what help can a classical Latin author provide? Virgil was a writer dear to Catholic Europe. The *Aeneid* had no sooner appeared after Virgil's death in 19 BCE that it became the canonical myth of Rome's origins. In the poem Virgil relates how Aeneas escaped from Troy after it had been sacked by the Greeks and, after years of wandering, reached Italy and settled in Latium, eventually the birthplace of the twins Romulus and Remus, who founded Rome. Rome became the seat of Christianity and the Roman Catholic Church; the *Aeneid* is a paean to Rome and its imperial destiny. But there was another reason why Virgil was important to Dante and the Catholic world. Virgil's Eclogue 4, which tells of the birth of a baby boy, a supposed saviour, was re-interpreted by Christian scholars to be a poem on the birth of Jesus Christ and a prophecy about the coming Messiah.

So it is that Virgil, an unknowing Christian adrift in the Christian afterworld, acts as Dante's guide through the submerged lives and unmapped shores of the afterlife. In one of the most famous pairings in Western literature, the two men go on their hazardous way through Hell, Virgil instructing Dante all the while on ethics, willpower and human mortality. For Dante and Virgil alike the going is tough. On entering the first circle of Hell after Charon has ferried them across the River Acheron (a river situated in the Hades of Greek mythology), Virgil turns suddenly pale. The pallor must be pale fear, Dante says to Virgil, but Virgil responds that pity is the cause. Virgil has been moved by pity at his own damned state as a non-Christian born in the 'time of the false and lying gods' (*nel tempo de li dèi falsi e bugiardi*). As a pagan he cannot accompany Dante beyond Purgatory. Only Beatrice ('a spirit more worthy than I am', says Virgil) can serve as a vehicle for redemption and bring Dante to a proper knowledge of his propensity for evil and capacity for good. The choice of a pagan poet to accompany a Christian poet through the afterlife ran counter to all medieval Christian convention. From the start Dante was determined to unsettle: today Italians might call him *uno scrittore scomodo* – 'a discomfiting writer'.

Dante's intention was to make Hell, Purgatory and Heaven real to the common man, and for the common man to journey with him towards salvation. Hell was no phantasmagoria of the mind. Dante wanted readers to recognize themselves in his unhappy souls who, weighted with different sins, lament without end the end they have come to. Literal-minded gossips were said to have pointed to Dante in the street and whispered that his unusually dark skin was proof of a journey made to the underworld. *'Eccovi l'uom ch' è stato all'Inferno!'* ('See, there's the man that was in Hell!'); his sun tan had to be the devil's own work. Dante's Hell is not supposed to be so very different from the world we know. Italo Calvino thought that Dante was mistakenly labelled a fantasist; he was a realist: 'I don't want to talk nonsense about Dante', he wrote to the literary critic Mario Motta in 1950, 'but it seems to me that Dante is not "infernal" or "paradisiacal" at all, given his concern for men as they are, here on this earth.'

Four simple words in the opening canto, *cammin di nostra vita* ('journey of our life'), serve to distinguish the *Inferno* from the bizarre travel literature that had preceded it in the Middle Ages. The literature is known today as the literature of *oltretomba,* or 'afterlife', and its spirit is with us still. The *Oltretomba* horror comics sold at newspaper kiosks across Italy today present an otherworld of flying monster-devils and satanic orgies not so unlike the fantasias and allegorical journeys from which Dante wished to distance himself. Importantly, Dante's journey is not his journey alone, but a journey where all humankind will acquire knowledge of the world.

The journey begins before dawn on Good Friday and ends a week later on Thursday of Easter week, thus coinciding with the liturgical recurrence of Christ's passion. Dante's genius was to match the journeying metaphor of Everyman with the Holy week leading to the crucifixion and resurrection. The spiritual quest that opens with the *Inferno* in April 1300 illustrates the fundamental promise of Christ: 'Those who believe in me, even though they die, will live' (John 11:25). That is partly why Dante referred to *The Divine Comedy* as 'sacred'. The modern reader may disagree with and even be flummoxed by Dante's Christian vision, but *The Divine Comedy* is inescapably a Roman Catholic work of art; it mirrors the Catholic profession of faith with its emphasis on examination of conscience, confession of faults, the making of a purpose of amendment and restitution. For mortals ensnared by drink, say, or a compulsion to narcotics, *The Divine Comedy* offers a design for life, and so a glimmer of hope. The poem contains very little that Catholicism (or, for that matter, Buddhism, Agnosticism, New Age Spiritualism, Islam, Judaism and Protestantism) has not advocated down the generations. The Catholic moral practice of submitting one's will unreservedly to a Higher Power (a 'power' that may or may not be God) squares with modern twelve-step spiritual recovery programmes. It is probable, indeed almost certain, that Dante wrote *The Divine Comedy* because he wanted to help himself – help anyone – find a way out of the narrow and darkened prison of a life gone bad. He was writing at a time when religion was the great centre around which all the passions and interests of mankind revolved. When St Paul wrote to the church in Corinth that he has had his struggles but learned from his weakness to rely more on Christ

(2 Corinthians 12:9–10), he is letting us know that vulnerability has opened him up to the grace of spiritual recovery. So it was with Dante. Like all great religious literature, *The Divine Comedy* is a conversion story. And it is complicated, as conversion stories always are. As we have seen, Dante's unrequited love for Beatrice had left him so weak that the slightest insensitive remark sank him further into despair. *The Divine Comedy,* he hoped, would enable his renewal. For the pious and believing Catholic his conversion is all too credible. At the end of it all, Dante will be able to stand up straight and restored; hallowed anew, he will be able to walk in the right path.

As Dante goes deeper into Hell, the more vivid and disgusting the punishments become. 'Gluttons' have to swallow quantities of sludge in a rain-drenched mire, much as they did in life the things they craved. The poem's gross and gloomy atmosphere stays vivid in the mind. Corrupted bankers, love cheats, negligent and corrupt rulers; the unabsolved, the indolent and the excommunicate: all are consigned to flame, befouled in shite or submerged in pitch. Always accompanied by Virgil, Dante encounters serpentine-haired viperish monsters, howling naked shades, and other tormented creatures. As a singer of otherworldly horror he still has no equal. The creation of the horrid and disgusting was, for Dante, a necessary part of the impulse towards grace and salvation that culminates in *Paradiso.* Satan, pungent and hairy-flanked, languishes in a kingdom of perpetual night.

The journey to the underworld is one of the most obsessively recurring stories of the Western imagination. In Book XI of Homer's *Odyssey,* Ulysses descends into the kingdom of the dead. There, he conjures a swarm of ghosts, among them an unburied friend, his aged mother, and the blind clairvoyant Tiresias (the 'old man with wrinkled female breasts' of T. S. Eliot's *The Waste Land*). Homer's epic comes down to us from the dawn of Western literature. The first printed edition of the *Odyssey* did not appear in Florence until 1488, a century and a half after Dante's death, therefore Dante never read Homer. Instead he took the story of Ulysses from Latin sources, among them Cicero, Seneca, Horace and – above all – the Roman poet Ovid, who recounts it in the *Metamorphoses*. Just as Homer's underworld would inform Virgil's vision of Hades, so Virgil's account became the model for all later Western geographies of Hell, Dante's among them.

There is no doubt that Dante saw something of himself in Ulysses. The Greek sailor-hero is alluded to twice in *Purgatorio* and at least once in *Paradiso*; there are multiple indirect references to Ulysses in both poems, while an entire canto of *Inferno* is dedicated to Ulysses. Homer applies two Greek words to his wandering hero – *pollà plankte* – which perhaps explain why Dante felt so close to Ulysses. They mean 'much erring', or 'driven to wander far and wide'. In Homer's epic telling, Ulysses endures ten years of war in Troy, another ten years of vagabondage and yearning for his wife, Penelope, before returning home to Ithaca. Like Ulysses, Dante withstands the toughest of human trials and solitude before reaching metaphorical dry land. Nevertheless, the account which he puts in Ulysses' own mouth of a last journey to the western limits of the Mediterranean (*Inferno* canto 26) has no known precedent in literature; it is Dante's own. Ulysses, instead of returning home to Ithaca and his wife and son, sails with his ageing ship's crew southwest beyond the equator into an empty ocean. Ominously, they are seen to sail in a direction towards the left. Towards the left, or on the left, signifies 'evil' in *The Divine Comedy;* to climb to Purgatory one goes to the right; to descend to Hell, to the left, that is to say, the 'sinister' side. (In Italian bars and restaurants today the lavatory is usually, in my experience, '*In fondo a sinistra*' – 'At the back on the left'.) Ulysses's ship never reaches dry land. The sea sucks Ulysses and his men under. Dante condemns Ulysses to Hell for his god-defiant arrogance

Woodcut diagram of Hell, from an early-sixteenth-century
Venetian edition of *The Divine Comedy*.

Quellanima lassu cha magior pena
Disel maestro eguida scariocto
chel capa dentro et fuor legtime mena
Egualtri due chanol capo disocto
quel che pende dal nero ciesso ebruto
meti come si torce et no si mocto
Laltre cassio che par si menbruto
ma la nocte resurge et oramai
e da partir che tuctauen uedduto
Omallui piacquel collo la uinchiai
et el prese del tenpo luogo et posce
et qn lali furna pertasiai
Ipiglio se ale uellute cosce
Diuello inuello giu discese poscia
tral folto pelo et le gelate cosce
Quando noi fiimo la doue la coscia
si uolgiappunto insul grosso dellanche
lo ducha con faticha et con angoscia

Dante and Virgil observing the fate of the Lustful in canto 34 of the *Inferno*.
Illustration by Priamo della Quercia from the mid-fifteenth-century.

in wishing to explore unknown lands and venture into the brink of the unknown. Can it be a sin to know? The love of knowledge – the desire to know and understand the world – was for Dante an overriding passion and a part of what it means to be human: *The Divine Comedy* is a supreme expression of that passion. Yet the Bible had warned against curious-minded individuals conducting investigations where they should not. ('For in much wisdom is much grief': Ecclesiastes.) The passion to know – Ulysses' presence in Hell obliges us to conclude – is dangerous. In tasting of the apple of knowledge, and daring to exercise his curiosity, Ulysses had sinned against the divine order of things and put divine laws to test. The same fatal wanderlust was taken up by Tennyson, himself an admirer of Dante, who imagined a hubris-tempting Ulysses dreaming of new frontiers. And not only Tennyson. Pete Brown, the lyricist on the psychedelic *Disraeli Gears* album by Cream, clearly also knew this Ulysses who had sailed fatally close to the wind. 'Tales of Brave Ulysses' rhapsodises the 'Sirens sweetly singing' as the voyager sails into dangerous waters.

The *Inferno* is, among other things, a gleeful dream of retribution. Sinners are accorded their proper place through a retributive law known as the *contrapasso*. This law (from the Latin *contra* and *patior*, 'suffer the opposite') was Dante's own interpretation of the biblical law of 'an eye for an eye'. The English word is something like 'retribution'. It states that every sin will find its equal and fitting punishment. In canto 20 of the *Inferno*, quack astrologers and false prophets can walk only backwards as their heads have been bent round 180 degrees. The twisted nature of their divination and their failed attempts to see into the future ('they could not see ahead of them') find expression in Dante's diabolic *contrapasso*, where the sin itself becomes the punishment, and the sinners shuffle backwards in order to go forward, gazing down at their buttocks. Dante's backwards-walking sinners fascinated Samuel Beckett; in his 1956 radio play *All That Fall* Mr Rooney announces: 'Let us go on backwards now a little, arsy-versy like Dante's damned.'

Very often Florentines are subjected to this harsh law. Of the seventy-nine lost souls encountered in the *Inferno*, thirty-two are Florentine and eleven Tuscan; *Purgatorio* counts only four Florentines; *Paradiso*, other than Beatrice, just three. On the basis of these numbers alone, *Inferno* may be accounted the most anti-Florentine book ever written. Dante's keen observing gaze lets no guilty Florentine go free; in their pitiable nakedness they even seem to exult in their sin. Ciacco (the word became Florentine slang for 'Pig' thanks to Dante), the first of the many Florentines seen in Hell, wallows luxuriantly in his own filth.

Whenever Dante meets a Florentine in *The Divine Comedy*, the painful subject of his exile is likely to arise. By dating the action to 1300, a couple of years before his banishment, Dante allows the dead to foresee all that will occur in the intervening two years and create an impression of prophetic power. In canto 17 of *Paradiso* his great-great-grandfather Cacciaguida foretells the poet's expulsion from Florence two years later, in 1302.

> You will leave behind every thing
> you hold most dear; and this is just the first
> arrow shot by your exile – your first wound.
> You will experience how terribly salty
> is the taste of another man's bread, and feel how hard
> going up and down another man's stairs is.

Dante had been in exile for fifteen years when he wrote those lines; recast imaginatively by W. B. Yeats in his poem 'Ego Dominus Tuus' the words express not only Dante's own pain at wandering but the sorrow of refugees the world over, in every age:

> Derided and deriding, driven out
> To climb that stair and eat that bitter
> bread…

The exile's bread will be expensive, and 'bitter', for Dante will have to beg for it. Cacciaguida is also warning that the bread his descendant will have to eat will be unpleasantly different. Tuscan bread even today is hard to find outside Tuscany as it contains no salt; called *pane sciocco* (literally 'daft bread'), it is best eaten as Dante would have eaten it in Florence – with olive oil.

*

Edward Said, in his celebrated 1978 book *Orientalism,* argued that Dante posits a crudely schematic view of the 'Christian West' versus the 'Muslim East'. Islam, geographically tied to the 'Orient', is made a target for popular anti-Arab and anti-Islamic apprehension. Is this true? In Dante's day, Islam was not some dark and far-distant East but a neighbouring presence that overlapped with the Christian world. We know that Islam was an active presence in Byzantium; one of the main gates of the Pisa city walls is named after an Arab merchant; and there are Arab influences in the architecture of the Duomo in Florence. Spain and Sicily, to the west and south of Dante's native Tuscany, had been under Muslim rule only a century earlier; inevitably there remained a strong Muslim presence in the Spanish and Sicilian courts of the late Middle Ages. Astronomical knowledge was essentially an Arab science in Dante's time. The Arab astronomer Alfragano (al-Farghānī) powerfully influenced Dante's imagination. His *Elementa Astronomica* (as the book is known in Latin) was Dante's astronomical handbook, and informed much of the planetary verse in *Paradiso*. Islam, far from being conflated by Dante with an Oriental 'Other', was actually very close to home.

The Prophet Muhammad is punished in canto 28 of the *Inferno* not as the founder of Islam, but as a 'sower of discord'. Muhammad was seen by Dante as a man diminished by a lust for temporal power. As a renegade from the 'true faith', moreover,

Muhammad had ruptured Christianity through preaching a *nuova legge* or 'new law'. Islam, for Dante, was an unfulfilled or *misfulfilled* manifestation of Christianity. The Prophet and his cousin Ali (later, after marrying Muhammad's daughter Fatima, his son-in-law) represent a schism. In the *Inferno* Ali's face is split in half, while the Prophet's torso is 'gutted from his chin down to the farting place'. The rending of the Christian church thus finds a corporal equivalent in Dante's sanguinary *contrapasso*, where the dividers of humanity are themselves divided. Ali himself is damned because he engineered a schism in orthodox Islam by founding the Shiite sect in the aftermath of the Prophet's death in AD 632. This split the caliphate of the Muslim community, and set Shiites against Sunnis. The Prophet's is a horrible punishment to be sure. A sword-bearing devil slashes open his wound whenever it heals itself. Dante's symbolism could hardly be more suggestive for our age, when sectarian violence between Sunnis and Shiites continues to open wounds in the body politic of the Middle East.

Edward Said does not seem to want to acknowledge that *all* schismatics, not just the Prophet and Ali, are subjected to violence in canto 28. One can understand why Said took Dante to task. In the allegorical Christian books and poems of Dante's day, Muslims are portrayed as primitive rebels against Christianity. The medieval French epic *Chanson de Roland* (Song of Roland), which Dante knew well, shows Muslims in obeisance to an unholy Trinity made up of the Prophet, the Greek god Apollo and a harsh-tempered female deity called the Termagant. In canto 18 of *Paradiso* Dante's illustrious forebear Cacciaguida, who died in the Holy Land during the disastrous (for Christians) Second Crusade of 1147–9, blames the very existence of Islam on a breakdown in 'pastoral care' within the Christian church. This does not make Muslims – that 'foul race' (*quella gente turpa*) – any the less deserving of vilification. Cacciaguida, whose pugnacious presence may serve as a counterweight to Beatrice, is representative of the vanished Florentine virtues (as Dante saw them) of honesty, simplicity and integrity. The exaltation of Cacciaguida among the blessed of *Paradiso* is predicated on his very martyrdom to the Christian cause against Muslim forces.

In canto 8 of the *Inferno* Dante approaches the city of Dis in Lower Hell. 'Dis', usually a name for Satan, is here imagined as an Islamic citadel. A mass of gleaming red towers like the Muslim desert towers in William Burroughs's 1981 novel *Cities of the Red Night* ('the whole northern sky lit up red at night...Dante's Inferno') emerges in the hazy distance. The towers are referred to as '*meschite*', mosques, and signify heretical allegiance and false faith. It is not surprising that *meschite* should be the only Arabic loanword in *The Divine Comedy* that refers to Islam: the Crusades were a recent memory to Dante's generation. Dante's parents were very much alive when Edward I of England took part in the seventh Crusade against Islam in 1248. In the medieval Christian judgment, mosques were the seat and symbol of a stubborn and erroneous belief.

For all that, Dante's was not an 'Orientalist' denigration of Islam. As we have seen, Occidental Islam was connected to the Italian peninsula by a long history of cultural exchange and tolerance. The Arabic influence was palpable in Sicily, where the seaport of Marsala had been named after the Arab *marsā lāh,* Harbour of God. (Marsala is famous today for its – notably un-Muslim – production of fortified wine.) Christian and Muslim learning had been equally welcome at the Palermitan court of the Holy Roman Emperor Frederick II, whose own poetry, for all its slightly laboured pomp, merged Provençal troubadour love song with an Arabic-Saracen *douceur*. One of the Frederician court poets admired by the younger Dante, Giacomo da Lentini, is mentioned in canto 24 of *Purgatorio* as the '*Notaro*' or Notary: he was a lawyer from the Sicilian city of Catania. Some forty poems by da Lentini have survived, most of them in the form that he was said to have invented: the sonnet. Dante freely admitted the influence of da Lentini and other Arabo-Sicilian vernacular poets such as Ciullo d'Alcamo and Rinaldo d'Aquino ('all the poems of our predecessors in the vulgar tongue were called Sicilian', he writes in *De vulgari.*) They represented a tradition of authentic knowledge and curiosity about Islam, which Dante shared.

Neither is Dante's punishment of the Prophet so cruel as to suggest a denigration of all Islam. At a time when European romances used the derogatory term 'Mahound' for Muhammad (in Islam dogs – hounds, a possible source for 'Mahound' – are reckoned to be a ritually unclean animal), Dante included three Muslim luminaries among the 'righteous unbaptized' of the *Inferno* (canto 4). The possibility of salvation for virtuous unbelievers was a view shared by the fourteenth-century English writer William Langland in *Piers Plowman,* and by the medieval armchair traveller Sir John Mandeville, whose work first circulated some forty years after *The Divine Comedy.* The respect that Dante accords the three Muslims suggests a covert sympathy for Islam and Arabic culture. He encounters them in the borderline Limbo zone of Hell for those who are not wicked enough for Hell but who are not yet redeemed enough for Heaven. They are: the twelfth-century Kurdish sultan of Egypt, Saladin (Salah al-Din), who defeated the Crusaders in 1187 and retook Jerusalem, the Andalucian philosopher Averroës (Ibn Rushd), whose Arabic commentaries on Aristotle were credited with the survival of Aristotelian philosophy in the West, and Avicenna (Ibn Sina), another noted medieval Muslim Aristotelian. The warrior-prince Saladin was renowned for the mercy he showed his captive Crusaders, while the philosophers Averroës and Avicenna deserve 'honour' (the word is used eight times of them by Dante) because they are scholars of 'great authority'. Dante had placed these three non-Christians in Limbo (alongside his beloved Aristotle, Homer, Ovid and Virgil himself) because he could not bear to damn them to Hell. They suffer no outward physical torment; no shame scorches them inside.

Early commentators on *The Divine Comedy* claimed the Prophet as an apostate Catholic cardinal who founded an offshoot of Christianity after his failure to be appointed pope. Dante is likely to have shared this medieval belief. Accompanied as usual by Virgil he is struck dumb at the sight of the butchered Prophet, who prises open his chest with his hands for Dante to see:

> The bowels hung out between his legs;
> one could see his organs and the foul sack
> that makes shit from all we swallow.
> I stood and stared at him –
> he gazed back, tearing open his chest
> with both hands. 'Look how Muhammed claws
> and mangles himself, torn open down to the breast!
> Ali goes screaming in front of me,
> carved from his chin down to his brow….'

Here, conceivably, is the Islamic legend of *al-sharh* or symbolic 'opening up' of Muhammad's breast by God with the intent to morally purify him. Only it is transformed by Dante into a scene of carnivalesque horror. Dante may have known that the Prophet Muhammad died on the same day as Beatrice – 8 June; if so, the coincidence would surely have dismayed him.

The subject of Dante and Islam has upset non-Muslims too. In 1919 a renowned Spanish Arabist and Roman Catholic priest, Miguel Asín Palacios, caused a furore when he argued in his book *Muslim Eschatology in the Divine Comedy* that the Florentine poet had not only borrowed from Muslim sources but been heavily influenced by Islamic eschatological tradition. Italian Dantists were mostly aghast: Dante's Christianity and very identity as a European had been undermined by Palacios's insistence on a debt to Islam. (Pointedly, Palacios's book was not published in Italy until 1993, seventy-four years after the Spanish original, *La éscatologia musulmana en la Divina Comedia.*) According to Palacios, Dante's poem is an elaboration of a nighttime journey which Muhammad undertook in AD 620 through the seven levels of Heaven before fathoming the depths of Hell. The journey, known in Arabic as the *Isra and Mi'raj* (The Night Visit and Ascension), is mentioned in the Koran. However, most details of the journey derive from the later oral traditions or *hadiths* surrounding the Prophet, and from the *Kitab al-Miraj* (Book of the Ascension), written in Arabic around the eleventh century. The Prophet's nocturnal adventure was instigated by the archangel Gabriel (Jibril), whose winged steed Buraq takes Muhammad from Mecca to the 'farthest mosque', usually understood to be the Temple Mount in Jerusalem. After alighting at Jerusalem the Prophet ascends by a golden ladder with Gabriel into heaven. At each of the seven levels of heaven he meets a different prophet; first Adam, then John the Baptist and Jesus, followed by Joseph, Idris, Aaron, Moses and, lastly, Abraham. Muhammad continues upwards until he communes with Allah and is then guided through Hell.

Aspects of the Prophet's miraculous night ride do seem to be echoed in *The Divine Comedy*. A guide (Gabriel) takes the pilgrim-voyager (Muhammad) on a tour through the afterlife. Hell, which, according to the *Kitab al-Miraj*, lies just beneath Jerusalem, echoes with the wailing sounds of woe and sundered lives. An ever-streaming multitude of sinners rolls into the night as the dead, shrouded or coffined fix Muhammad with a viper glare. Paradise, by contrast, has springs, rivers, a purifying fire and a bright, almost inhuman luminosity. The Prophet even visits a part of the Islamic Hell reserved for those 'who sow discord'. Dante (though obviously in a spirit of sacrilege) placed Muhammad in just such a slough of 'schismatics'. The rewards of Heaven – emeralds, pearls, gold, silver – are moreover emphasized in the Arabic book as they are in *Paradiso*, with its promise of 'rubies' and the 'cool refreshment of an eternal shower' (*lo refregerio dell'etterna ploia*).

Persian miniature from the mid-1500s. Muhammad's night journey and ascension to Heaven. The Prophet sits astride his miraculous horse Buraq, encircled by angels.

پنج شنبه آیه تدبیر و کریم کلام
طوق آمد آن طوق کند ته دست
لبیک علوی حرام حرمت جاری
زین پایه ره و تدبیر ورد در
گرده رطوق کند نه دست
چون و راور و رخین علی پای
این دیوان ر و رو بصرت ور
شد و نقش نه رولوش نه بر
تابیریش پرو آیا نه بت
و و این بر ماشین کهو ر
در شب تیر آن پیران میر
برق کر داد پر بری رو پشت

لرجال الذين يغتابون المسلمين عند الظالمين ليأخذوا أموالهم بال

والذين يرمون الفتن بين المسلمين ٥

All the same, Dante's borrowings are not easy to prove. What we do know is that the *Kitab al-Miraj* was translated into Castilian in the mid-thirteenth century by a Hispano-Jewish physician named Abraham 'Alfaquím' (*al-hakīm*, in Arabic, 'the doctor' or 'wise one'). It was subsequently printed in Castilian – one cannot say published – as the *Book of Muhammad's Ladder*. A golden ladder of light enables Muhammad to begin his ascent to Paradise. The Castilian translation (no longer extant) served as the basis for both the Latin *Liber scale Machometi* and the Old French *Livre de l'eschiele Mahome,* which appeared between 1260 and 1264. Both translations were the work of the Italian lawyer-poet Bonaventura of Siena, an exiled Tuscan Ghibelline whose patron was King Alfonso X of Castile.

There are several ways in which Dante might have seen Bonaventura's Latin and French translations. The most likely is through his mentor Brunetto Latini, who between 1259 and 1260 served in Seville as Florentine ambassador to Alfonso X. Known as 'the Learned', Alfonso was a cultivated sovereign who encouraged the translation of Arabic works into Castilian vernacular. Either Latini heard stories of Muhammad's night voyage from Alfonso X, which he then communicated to Dante, or Latini presented Dante with a copy of the Castilian *Book of the Ladder of Muhammad.*

It is certain that Islamic culture flowed into Italy through al-Andalus (Muslim Spain). Though Dante never spent time in Spanish Muslim lands and (as far as we know) spoke no Arabic, Latini was immersed in Arabo-Andalusian intellectual life. In 1264 he was certainly in Cordoba. Very likely he travelled on to the Andalusian capital of Granada, where the red-coloured Alhambra (*Kalat al-Hamra,* 'Red Castle') would soon be built. In Granada the Moorish-Andalusian architecture, with its cedarwood ceilings and jasper arches, stood as a reminder of those tolerant times before King Ferdinand and Queen Isabella expelled Muslims from

The Prophet Muhammad on a tour of the infernal world. Sinners who have falsely denounced the apostles of Islam are pierced by devils with swords. From a fifteenth-century manuscript of the *Kitab al-Miraj.*

Spain in the late fifteenth century. Latini's two years in medieval Iberia coincided with the peaceful 'coexistence' (*convivencia,* in Spanish) of Islam with Christianity. In Seville, where Latini was based, the interior of the Almohad Mosque with its gold mosaic tesserae gave an overwhelming impression of luminosity and purity of spatial volume. Its geometric harmonies, intimating things beyond the comprehension of man, were an exploration of Islamic notions of infinity; the divine spheres, shining circles and heavenly roses of Dante's *Paradiso* issue from the same monotheistic belief system.

Latini's diplomacy at the Alfonsine court in Seville could not save him from Hell. Condemned to the seventh circle among the 'sodomites' of canto 15, he emerges from a vast desert of sterile sand on which flames unceasingly rain, suggesting a reversal of nature: fire usually burns upwards. Latini has been in Hell for six years by the time Dante is reunited with him. Doomed to perpetual movement to keep his feet from burning he greets his old pupil with pleasure ('How marvellous!'), addressing him as 'my son'. There is no guile or deceitfulness in Latini's fatherly greeting; his face, charred by cinders that float hot on the air, astonishes his former pupil:

> And I – as he stretched out his arm to me –
> gazed so hard at his scorched appearance
> that his burnt features could not prevent
>   me from realizing that this was one I truly knew.

The encounter, one of the most famous in *The Divine Comedy,* was present to T. S. Eliot when he came to write the 'Little Gidding' section of *Four Quartets.* Eliot's purgatorial poem, written in unrhymed Dantescan *terza rima,* is set at dusk in a desolate London landscape following a German bomb attack. It was written in 1941–2 after London and provincial British cities had been blitzed continuously, and all over England the skyline was lit red. Life as Eliot had known it, lived it and loved it, was gravely threatened. The poem unfolds amid the dust and parched ground of a bomb-torn street (probably Cromwell Road, where Eliot then worked as a firewatcher); the stench of burned buildings, compact of blackened masonry, dust and pitch, hangs heavy on the air:

> In the uncertain hour before the morning
> Near the ending of interminable night
> At the recurrent end of the unending…

As Eliot picks his way along the 'silent' pavement he encounters a ghost-like stranger alternately 'walking' and 'loitering' in shadow. Eliot looks searchingly at the stranger's face. He is aware that this is someone he knows but it takes a while before he is able to identify him. He is a long-dead (but dimly recollected) 'master'. To the shade Eliot calls out: 'What! Are *you* here?' It is the moment when Dante catches sight of Latini in Hell: '*Siete voi qui, Ser Brunetto?*' (The question is asked in the second person plural, the archaic respectful form.)

'Are *you* here, Sir Brunetto?'

The London ghost, a compound, according to Eliot, of Yeats, Mallarmé and Swift (though Milton seems also to be eerily present), is charged with a sense of transitoriness and loss; presumably hoping to find some meaning in the deaths and the full horror of what military technology could visit on civilization, Eliot watches as the man with the lined, brown face vanishes into the smoke.

> The day was breaking. In the disfigured street
> He left me, with a kind of valediction,
> And faded on the blowing of the horn.

The penalty for Latini's presumed 'sin' – homosexuality – is painful for Dante to behold. In medieval Christianity, homosexuality was classified, not as a sin of incontinence or weakness of will (as lust was), but as a sin against nature. His head bowed low with reverence and love, Dante acknowledges to Latini that it was he who 'taught me how man makes himself immortal' (*l'uom s'etterna*), immortality presumably referring here to writerly fame. The praise sits uncomfortably with the manner of Latini's damnation. This was not simply an encounter of a pupil with his master, but the encounter of a generation with its intellectual mentor. The men show great respect and affection for each other. Latini's sternly passive fortitude in dealing with his torment only increases his nobility in our eyes; in Latini's baffled pride Dante sees a rare dignity. As Latini runs off to rejoin his group of wrongdoers over the sand charred red by heat, Dante compares him to a runner in the Veronese palio horse race. Robert Lowell, in his translation of canto 15, from his 1967 poetry collection *Near the Ocean*, communicates Latini's pride:

> Then he turned back, and he seemed one of those who run for the green cloth through the green field at Verona… and seemed more like the one who wins the roll of cloth than those who lose

Like Ulysses, Latini is neither straightforwardly condemned nor seen to have gone very grievously astray. (At any rate he is not the palio's last man in.) This is hardly conventional Christianity. Dante seems to want to grant Latini's soul the grace of inspiration and healing. At some level, the poet identified with this outcast wandering Hell in penury and exile.

But there is also this to be said. Dante displays no prurience in his depiction of the sodomites of the seventh circle. Was Latini even 'guilty' of the perceived 'crime'? Latini is known to have spoken out against sodomy as '*contra natura*'. No great charge is laid against him in the canto, yet it is among the sodomites that Dante encounters him. Florence in Dante's day may have acquired a reputation as a sodomitical hotbed (by the early sixteenth century, a German dictionary defined a 'Florenzer' as a 'buggerer'), yet there is no recorded evidence that Latini engaged in sexual activities that the Catholic Church would have condemned. The best we can surmise is that some sort of failure of will or reason had led to Latini being exiled from human nature. Perhaps Latini had failed to repent before he died. If he had, he would have been accorded God's grace and, after an apprenticeship in Purgatory, entered Paradise. Sin is often ambiguous and many-faceted in Dante's work; the sinner may have virtues as well as faults. And Latini, who died in 1293, exemplifies such ambiguity.

The great absent figure in the *Inferno* is Guido Cavalcanti. All the same his memory hangs like a black cloud over canto 10. Cavalcanti is one of two poets to be named and discussed in Hell – a negative privilege. (The other, in canto 28, is the twelfth-century troubadour Bertan de Born.) Cavalcanti is spoken of by his father, Cavalcante de' Cavalcanti, who languishes amid flames on the outskirts of Dis among the heretics or Epicureans. Epicureanism had been popular in Florence with the Ghibellines but a taste for this kind of Greek philosophy was reckoned dangerous. Epicurus had denied the immortality of the soul: there is no personal life beyond the grave (we fall asleep and never awake again), so pleasure must be taken in the here and now. Dante seems to want to give the Epicureans Hell. By rights, 'Guido' the poet himself cannot be in Hell because he died four months after *The Divine Comedy*'s fictional April date of Easter 1300. He already has one foot in the underworld, however, and Dante writes of him with foreknowledge of his future fate. Whatever is going to happen has already happened.

In a vast cemetery strewn with the burning sarcophagi of the heretics Dante picks his way accompanied by Virgil. The tombs, open for the present, will be sealed for eternity after the Day of Judgment. Sunk in fire, a heretic recognizes Dante's Tuscan accent. (Even today, spoken Tuscan is distinguished by its

absence of the c and q sound, so that *seconda* becomes *sehonda*, for example, or *questa*, *huesta*, and, to the amusement of tourists, Coca Cola, Hoha Hola.) Dante is afraid, but Virgil urges him to approach to the tomb. The heretic turns out to be Farinata degli Uberti, a leader of the Tuscan Ghibellines, and therefore Dante's political enemy. In a parody of the risen Christ Farinata stands upright in the furnace of his tomb: the flames recall the fire to which heretics were condemned. His manner, dignified and august, suggests that he is piqued by his damned state. With disdain in his voice Farinata is drawn into an argument with Dante about Guelf–Ghibelline discord, which Dante wins by pointing out that the Guelfs eventually expelled the Ghibellines from Florence. Farinata is interrupted by another shade, who rises out of the same lidless sarcophagus. This is Cavalcante de' Cavalcanti, who, like his poet son Guido, had been suspected of atheism. He looks round anxiously, as though searching for someone, then, weeping, asks Dante: '*mio figlio ov' è? e perchè non è teco?*' 'Where's my son? Why isn't he here with you?' (The thin, whining tones of the repeated vowel 'e' in the Italian are brilliantly evocative of a querulous old man.) Why is Guido not with Dante? Dante replies:

'I don't come on my own:
that one waiting there will guide me,
I hope, to one your Guido had perhaps despised.'

In other words: Virgil is taking Dante to Beatrice, who, in turn, will take him on to the 'despised' God in heaven. An ideological falling-out with Guido over religion seems to be hinted at here; but what prompts old man Cavalcante to despair is not religion, but a simple matter of syntax. To Dante he shouts back:

'What did you say? he "*had*"? Can he be dead?
Doesn't sweet light touch his eyes?'

Dante's innocent use of the past tense 'had' (*ebbe*) implies that Guido is no longer alive. Cavalcante, his hopes wrecked, sinks back into the tomb and is heard of no more. Afterwards, Farinata resumes his conversation with Dante, prophesying, among other things, his imminent exile from Florence. Though Farinata is Guido Cavalcanti's father-in-law, he shows no interest in the poet's fate. Instead he explains how he and other damned Epicureans are able to foresee the future but have no knowledge of the present. Dreadfully, Cavalcante can *see* into the future – and in that future his son Guido is dead; in the present, however, Guido is alive. The precise date of Guido Cavalcanti's death was established by the nineteenth-century Tuscan scholar Isidoro Del Lungo: 29 August 1300, sixteen weeks after *The Divine Comedy's* time frame ends. Cavalcante's agony is that he knows the past where his son was alive, but he cannot know the present. At every moment he is condemned to uncertainty over his son's fate.

This justly famous canto, so intensely dramatic, preoccupied Antonio Gramsci for more than twenty years. The Sardinian theoretician of Italian Marxism had studied Dante during his student days in pre-First World War Turin, and continued into the early 1930s as he worked hard on his notebooks and letters in various Fascist-controlled clinics and prisons. Gramsci was thirty-five when, in 1926, Fascist police had arrested him as leader of the Italian Communist Party. Losing his sight but not his political faith, Gramsci underwent his own journey through a kind of Hell in incarceration. He filled a total of thirty-three notebooks with sketches for ideas in order to prove to himself that he was still alive and not in a dark wood. In canto 10 Dante compares Hell to a 'blind prison' (*cieco carcere*); Cavalcante's 'blindness' to everything immediately present to him combined with his 'limpid clarity' (as Gramsci calls it) about the future was a peculiarly refined torment.

Gramsci's magnificent fifteen-page essay on canto 10, published in his posthumous *Prison Notebooks*, serves as a springboard for deeper considerations of the political blindness of Mussolini's Italy. Gramsci disliked the arid academicism of much Dante scholarship under Fascism; numerous so-called scholars ('intellectual ruffians', Gramsci calls them) are berated for their seeming ineptitude. The essay is distinguished by its moral empathy for old man Cavalcante, whose 'paternal tenderness' (*tenerezza paterna*) towards his son Guido conceivably struck a chord with Gramsci as a father himself. The agony of doubt and uncertainty that afflicts the father before he must conclude – mistakenly – that Guido is dead moved Gramsci profoundly. In his reading, the damnation of Cavalcante belonged to an 'enormous' historical moment in Europe when prophets, augurers, prestidigitators, soothsayers, divinators and other far-seeing individuals were punished as witches, often by blindness. They had spent their lives looking the wrong way for the meaning of men's affairs; now they must regret their frustrated lives in Hell.

Gramsci died on 27 April 1937, the public prosecutor of his trial having said of him: 'We must stop this man's brain working for twenty years.' Mussolini's fascist regime had decided that Gramsci was a danger to the state. It is appropriate that Gramsci should lie buried in Rome's English cemetery, a few tombs away from the Romantic, proto-socialist 'red' poet Percy Bysshe Shelley, one of Dante's finest English translators. The drowsy, anemone-strewn graveyard – so unlike the flaming boneyard where Dante stumbles on Cavalcante – could almost be a churchyard in the English home counties, were it not for the cypresses and cicadas. 'It might make one in love with death', declared Shelley, 'to be buried in so sweet a place'.

Photo portrait of Antonio Gramsci, the philosopher and grand theoretician of Italian Marxism, taken in 1916.

Purgation

'And every creature shall be purified'
CHRISTOPHER MARLOWE, *Dr Faustus*

'Man, slow down, don't walk so fast
All you got to do is take your time
We'll get there
Stay in the road'
CHAMPION JACK DUPREE, *Strollin'*

At the end of the *Inferno*, Dante and Virgil climb down Satan's body and out past his great reeking feet to a tunnel that will conduct them to a purgatorial in-between land and, eventually, to Paradise regained. Dante has seen all there is of human sin by the time he reaches the poem's purgatorial place of repentance and regeneration. If the dark wood of the *Inferno* represented the state of sin into which Dante had fallen after Beatrice died, *Purgatorio* represents the moral perfection that should be aspired to in life.

It is a bright Easter Sunday morning pervaded by a quickened sense of life. The lungs fill with clean air, the grass is green underfoot and the sky shines serene overhead. Dante has left behind the filth and horror of the infernal realm in order to embark on 'better waters' (*migliori acque*). Purgatory is not mentioned in the Bible but it was widely believed in medieval Italy that it was located in Sicily on the summit of Mount Etna, the volcano. Perhaps with this topography in mind, Dante imagines Purgatory as a great conical mountain rising from the sea into the sunshine and up towards God. Purgatory envisaged in this way was a departure from most traditions of the time. Medieval authors located this Tolkien-like Middle Kingdom underground, often inside a deep cave; for Dante, however, Purgatory was a halfway house between Heaven and earth that looked skywards towards grace. The shores of Mount Purgatory on to which the poet and his 'leader' Virgil emerge are described in tones of the romantic melancholy that Shelley so admired.

> We then came out across a solitary shore
> that never saw its waters navigated
> by any man who knew how to return.

Dante, standing on the shores of the island of Mount Purgatory, is dazzled by a white light approaching from across the sea:

> And, having briefly drawn my eyes away
> To ask my leader what this light could be,
> I found it now grown greater and more bright.

The light, a spooky evanescence, shimmers like the 'star-seeped milky flowing mystic sea' of Arthur Rimbaud's poem 'The Drunken Boat'. It emanates from an angel, who is propelling a boat along with its beating wings; in the boat are the souls of the Redeemed. Dante's gift for invention in *Purgatorio* is remarkable. From Homer to Rimbaud to J. G. Ballard, one of the functions of great literature has been to invoke believable 'other worlds'. In his 1962 novel *The Drowned World* Ballard turned London into a seething jungle swamp; afterwards in *The Crystal World* he petrified the world into a subtropical crystalline forest. The hallucinated clarity and strangeness of Ballard's imagery was in its own way Dantean: *Purgatorio* is distinguished by its imaginative strangeness as Dante writes with the curiosity of a foreigner captivated by everything new. Already at the start of the canticle we are in an other-worldly realm. Sapphire hues 'from the Orient' mark out the nine ledges or cornices (*cornice*, Dante calls them) of Mount Purgatory. At the mountain's summit is the Earthly Paradise, a charmed and temperate space traversed by crystal streams.

In some ways, too, *Purgatorio* is a travel narrative; Dante has journeyed through the horror-zone of Hell, just as Chaucer and his pilgrim crew would soon afterwards make the (somewhat easier) London to Canterbury tour under the guidance of a raucous innkeeper. Appropriately, *peregrinus*, the medieval term for a 'pilgrim' or 'traveller', in classical Latin meant an 'exile' or 'alien'. Dante's Hell had been presented as a place of exile, where a dreadful night hung over all. The inhabitants had longed for the daylight world; but, amid the spectacle of flames and the foul stinking pits, they were unable to move. Hell is the absence of God; sin, in Dante's stern morality, imprisons.

Repentance is the only reason why the people in Purgatory are not in Hell. In Ante-Purgatory at the foot of the mountain are those souls who repented too late or who died outside the church. Their sufferings may seem as terrible as those of the damned (they can only begin the process of purgation once they have waited 'thirty times as long' as they lived a heedless life on earth), but they willingly submit to the sufferings, as they are a means to salvation. Purgatory, in the medieval belief, is a Hell of limited duration, where the stain of sin can be removed through a series of cleansing torments. Penitents who opportunely turned to God at the moment of their death are heard singing the Miserere Domine psalm which invokes God's forgiveness. Among them are Manfred, the illegitimate son of Frederick II of Sicily, and the Ghibelline general Buonconte da Montefiore, a bad man who at the close of his life sincerely repented.

In *Purgatorio*, Dante is himself a penitent among penitents. He purges himself of wrongful desires, or rather of the traces that wrongful desires and actions have left in him. Perhaps we all of us need to journey into a pit before we can see the light, Dante seems to be saying. The poem teems with souls who are in the process of learning from each other and flourishing as they acquire deeper self-knowledge and self-awareness, and rediscover the human capacity for happiness. The souls change as we read about them, indeed they are destined to change because sin is not seen by Dante as an ineradicable disease, but rather as a misconception or perversion of love. Importantly, these souls help Dante in his own spiritual and physical recovery. They view themselves as a community, a fellowship, whose suffering, praying and singing is done together. (In Hell, by contrast, there is no sense of a community, only a horrid confusion without end and without redemption.) Social interactions in Purgatory are intended to be a model of how life should be on earth; it is a place where people behave as they should behave in life.

Still darkly troubled by his past sins (and, of course, by the moral disorder of Florence), Dante follows Virgil across a lonely plain, 'like one who returns to the road he has lost'. Outwardly, *Purgatorio* is the most philosophical of the poem's three books. Virgil discourses here on the nature of *virtù* (moral virtue), and the relationship between body and soul; biblical quotation coexists with quotation from Aristotle, Plato and Aquinas. Discussions, both formal and precise, are held on the efficacy of prayer and the nature of love. *Purgatorio* is also oddly human. At the base of Mount Purgatory Virgil washes Dante's face with morning dew (a scriptural image of divine mercy). The gesture is one of many which lend a near-domestic quality to *Purgatorio*, a quality of the life we live and know. An atmosphere of rue and penitence, of prayer and spiritual aspiration, intensifies as Dante ascends the mountain. As always in Dante, sin or vice is seen as the result of poor judgment; such a view of human experience at least allows for moral perfectibility or, in theological terms, 'healing grace' (*gratia sanans*). It will take Dante three days to reach the top of the mountain.

In the course of his ascent he will learn how the 'crooked way' can be made straight, and the 'fog of the world' (*la caligine del mondo*) purged away. The journey is cast as a return to Beatrice and the moral and spiritual inspiration she bestowed on Dante after his desolating passion for her had at long last receded. On first entering Purgatory proper in canto 9 the poet's forehead is inscribed with seven 'P's by a sword-bearing angelic gatekeeper. In Latin the word for sin is *peccatum*. The seven sins (*peccati*, in Italian) will be erased one by one as Dante reaches the end of each of the cornices. As the penitential 'P's of Envy, Gluttony, Greed, Avarice, Lust, Pride, Sloth and Wrath are erased, so Dante's progress upwards becomes easier. With the keys of St Peter – one gold and one silver – the angels open the Gate of Purgatory. As the gate opens, Dante hears a heavenly chorus from the Te Deum Laudamus: God, We Praise You.

Among the souls on the lowest slopes of Purgatory is the medieval troubadour poet Sordello da Goito (the hero of Robert Browning's poem 'Sordello'). The Mantua-born Sordello escorts Dante and Virgil to a shallow dip in the mountainside where they pass their first night. Progress up Mount Purgatory always has to stop when darkness falls, and divine grace (the light of the sun) is temporarily extinguished. In the course of his purgatorial travel (from the French *travail*, 'hard work' or 'penance'), Dante encounters two other vernacular poets. These are Guido Guinizelli, a founder of the *dolce stil novo*, and Arnaut Daniel, a Provençal near-contemporary of Sordello. The poets are purging themselves of sin on the cornice of Purgatory reserved for the lustful. (For the medieval mind, oddly, lust was the least heinous of crimes.) Arnaut speaks to Dante in a courtly Provençal: it is the only instance in the entire *Divine Comedy* where a non-Italian speaks in his mother tongue. Arnaut Daniel's technical superiority is acknowledged by Guinizelli, who terms him *il miglior fabbro del parlar materno* ('the better smith of the mother tongue'), a phrase which T. S. Eliot took up six centuries later as an epigraph to *The Waste Land* in order to honour Ezra Pound. Daniel's words are followed by praise to the virgin moon goddess Diana, who upheld the virtue of chastity by expelling one of her nymphs on learning that she was pregnant.

In canto 27, Dante must himself pass into the fire that purges the lustful. Purification by fire is a familiar image in scripture: 'He is like a refiner's fire' (Malachi, 3:2). Afterwards Dante spends his third and final night on Mount Purgatory. The canto already has an atmosphere of *Paradiso* and prepares us for heaven. We have emerged from the 'stage of punishment' (as T. S. Eliot called it) and the dark and bewildering world of temptation. At this point, with curiously little fanfare, Virgil takes leave of Dante, leaving Dante distraught. Before Virgil starts on the journey back to Limbo (where, as a pagan spirit, he resides) he addresses Dante:

> No longer look to me for words or signs.
> Your will is free, straight and whole.
> And not to follow its direction would be a fault.
> Lord of yourself, I crown and mitre you.

Soon after, Dante finds himself in a 'holy forest' (*divina foresta*), whose supernatural streams and rains contrast with the unknown dangers of the *selva oscura* (dark wood) where his journey had begun a week earlier. Forest (*foresta*) and wood (*selva*) were not semantically interchangeable in Dante's day. A wood was a place of wildness and dark supernatural fear; forest, the antithesis of woodland, was a controlled and carefully nurtured space, cognate with the Latin *foris*, 'outdoors' or 'outside': Dante's *foresta* is a delicious outdoor garden. We are in fact now in the Earthly Paradise, the biblical Garden of Eden by another name. If we look back, we can see that Dante has reached the 'delectable mountain' (*dilettoso monte*) which he had struggled to climb ninety-five cantos earlier, when his way was blocked by the leopard, she-wolf and lion. Here on the peak of Mount Purgatory he encounters a young woman, Matelda (usually mistranslated in English as 'Matilda'), who briefly takes over the role of Virgilian guide, heralding the approach of Beatrice. With her manifest beauty, Matelda appears to be the embodiment of earthly moral perfection and is associated (as was Beatrice in the *Vita nuova*)

overleaf
The Meeting of Dante and Beatrice in Purgatory by the Florentine painter Andrea Pierini, 1853. Beatrice's chariot is pulled by a gryphon.

with 'May-things in abundance' and a sense of renewal. Like a Golden World shepherdess she sings blithely to herself while choosing flowers to pluck but, tantalizingly, she does so on the far side of a stream from Dante. The stream is made up of Lethe, the classical waters of oblivion, and Eunoe, the fifth river of the dead, an invention of Dante's. Lethe runs to the right, Eunoe to the left.

After some conversation with Matelda about the nature of the place, a 'divine pageant' materializes. Figures representing the Ten Commandments, the forty-six books of the Catholic Old Testament and the seven gifts of the Holy Spirit process in stately grandeur along the stream's far bank. In the rear is the chariot of the church, drawn by the half-eagle, half-lion figure of the gryphon, representing the twin nature of Jesus as God and man. The chariot is flanked by female figures representing various theological and moral virtues. On the chariot rides a red-robed, green-mantled Beatrice, Dante's 'God-bearing image', to use the critic Charles Williams' memorable phrase.

Not by sight, but by the strange unrest in his blood does Dante understand who this woman is. The encounter is profoundly shocking and unexpected. Dante has not seen Beatrice for ten years: we might expect a moment of joyous reunion. Instead, at this climactic moment she explains to the angels surrounding her why she needs to be harsh in her treatment of Dante. Beatrice here is a very assertive, even jealous woman, quite unlike the Beatrice who inspired the Pre-Raphaelite artist and poet Dante Gabriel Rossetti to paint his lachrymose 'Beata Beatrix'. The nature of the failings for which Beatrice ferociously upbraids Dante is not specified, but most likely they have to do with infidelity. Beatrice had kept Dante on the right path during her brief life, but he cravenly abandoned her, sinking into such a moral dissipation that it brought him to the edge of death. Beatrice's acid taunt that Dante had 'yielded to another's glance' may refer to the *donna gentile* who offered consolation in the *Vita nuova*. In regal tones she upbraids Dante as a 'mother' might 'her son'.

> What right had you to climb to the mountain?
> Did you not know that all are happy here?

Though racked by shame and confusion Dante summons the courage to speak.

> Weeping, I said: 'Mere things of here and now
> and their false pleasures turned my steps away
> as soon as your face had gone from sight'.

Is that *it*? Beatrice continues to dress down and rebuke the untrustworthy man. Was it so clever of him to wait to be 'stricken by some girl' or other 'novelty of short-lived use'? Dante's selfishness had devastated what little dignity remained to him. Her harsh, outspoken displeasure encourages Dante to stop feeling sorry for himself. As he approaches the shores of Lethe he hears the words from Psalm 51 used by priests in absolution after confession. *Asperges me* – 'Sprinkle me (that I may be clean)'. In a form of baptism, Dante is then immersed in Lethe and afterwards recovers the memory of the few good deeds he has done on earth. Close up he can now see the gryphon reflected in Beatrice's eyes. The only way to save Dante from a life of blank nothingness and absorption in his own selfishness had been to send him on this journey, Beatrice's presence suggests – a journey which he has now more than half completed. Now the pilgrim must prepare himself to return to the temporal world that 'lives all wrong', and speak of what he has seen for the moral benefit of fellow men. But first he must ascend further into the precincts of light.

In the Precincts of Light

'Going to Heaven!
I don't know when –
Pray do not ask me how!'
                    EMILY DICKINSON, 'Going to Heaven!'

'How Much Longer Shall I Be Able to Inhabit The Divine'
                    TED BERRIGAN, Sonnet II

After his reunion with Beatrice on Mount Purgatory, Dante is 'ready to ascend to the stars'. He travels with his own body through Paradise, landing as he does so on all the solid bodies (planets) of the heavens, among them the Moon, Mercury and Venus, the Sun, Mars, Jupiter and Saturn. For most of his ascent Dante is accompanied by Beatrice, who smiles with delight as she explains that, once free of the "impediment" of sin, such levitation is only natural. On entering the sphere of Saturn Dante sees Jacob's ladder rising to the highest heavens, the Empyrean, situated at the summit of the medieval cosmos. On Mars Dante encounters his great-great-grandfather Cacciaguida; in the Heaven of Fixed Stars, the biblical Adam. Such scenes, verging on the comical, are at the very limit of what we can imagine to be possible. When Dante conjured and wrote them down he was a man in his early fifties humiliated by his dependence on patrons and his dignity still devastated by exile. *Paradiso*, begun in Ravenna in around 1316, was intended by Dante to give his life a final meaning and justification.

Virgil may have disappeared from Dante's side but the Roman poet's Classical culture continues to provide Dante with a source of elevated rhetoric. He enters *Paradiso* amid a flood of light:

> The glory of Him who moves all things
> penetrates the universe and shines
> in one part more and, in another, less.

A quest for the perfect lightness of being, *Paradiso* presents a world of startling illuminations and darting movements across vast, sidereal spaces, where a liquid light shines and shifts about Dante in every kind of dazzlement, from sun-smitten diamonds to solar lucencies. 'I have seen things which cannot be told', Dante announces to the reader. Dante is trying to describe a world made up of God's super-radiant light, a universally diffusive light without shadow. In canto 30 the Creator radiates a bright, liquid effluence:

> I envisaged light in the form of a rushing stream,
> resplendent with brightness, pouring between two banks
> painted with all the marvels of spring.
> And radiating from this torrent were live sparks
> which everywhere settled in the flowers,
> almost like rubies set in gold –
> then, as if intoxicated with the perfumes,
> they plunged again into the wondrous swirl;
> And as one sank in, another whirled out.

While everything on earth is subject to an awful brevity, in the celestial kingdom all is immutable and eternal. Dante's shimmering imagery of rays, astral sparks, radiances, fires and flames looks forward to the visionary verse of Rimbaud's *Illuminations*, where all is transcendence and aesthetic delectation. Just as Rimbaud intones, seer-like, of the cathedral he has glimpsed floating at the bottom of a lake, so Dante soars upwards beyond the human realm through the planets and out to the stars. *Paradiso* effectively changed the language of poetry. The verse, much of it, seems to delight in its own artifice, and approaches a mystique of art for its own sake. John Sinclair's 1939 prose translation of *Paradiso* captures the visionary Rimbaldian tone, where the verse matches the strange sublimity of the vision it describes. From canto 13:

A scene from canto 3 of Dante's *Paradiso*, mid-1400s, as depicted in a gleaming, jewel-like miniature by the Sienese artist Giovanni di Paolo. The image shows the encounter between Dante and the spirits of the nuns Piccarda Donati (sister of the

poet Forese Donati) and Costanza d'Altavilla (mother of Frederick II). On the right, Narcissus is inspecting his own image in a well. On Dante's chest is an image of the sun of love.

For I have seen the briar first show harsh and rigid all through
the winter and later bear the rose upon its top, and once I saw a
ship that ran straight and swift over the sea through all its
course perish at the last entering the harbour.

Paradiso can make unusually taxing demands on our pa-
tience and understanding. (To T. S. Eliot the poem was either
intensely exciting or wholly incomprehensible.) Doctrinal
discussions on the misuse of free will, the Creation, the Trinity,
the Incarnation, Atonement and Resurrection, the properties
of light and the workings of the medieval cosmos frustrate easy
comprehension. Beatrice's convoluted explanation in canto 2 of
the spots on the moon - are they the result of varying densities
in the same material, or of differing *types* of material? – needled
Samuel Beckett, for one. "I've been reading *Il Paradiso* and trying
again to understand Beatrice's explanation", he wrote in 1958 to his
friend Mary Hutchinson: the moon spot conundrum had baffled
Beckett since at least the mid-1930s. Of course, the science that
informs Dante's vision of the planets has long been discredited,
but it was the optimum science of Dante's time. In attempting
to elucidate the workings of the cosmos he brought difficult
ideas down a level (*haute vulgarisation,* the French would later
call it: 'high-class popularisation'). In *Paradiso* Dante displays a
polymath's enthusiasm and sense of wonder at the mysteries of
the physical world and a delight in extracting order out of chaos.
The more we know of the planetary systems, Dante seems to be
saying, the greater can only be our wonder at the divinely created
universe.

Every one of the poem's thirty-three cantos contains within
itself a model of the universe or an attribute of the universe:
infinity, time eternal, time present, time cyclic. The price Dante
pays for this theological and astronomical erudition is at times
a lack of human involvement. Samuel Johnson's complaint that

in *Paradise Lost* 'the want of human interest is always felt' is one that could also be levelled at the Dante of *Paradiso*, yet so could one of Johnson's resounding tributes to Milton: 'He…delighted to form new modes of existence'. Difficulty has its own rewards in *Paradiso*. Its bright, experimental orchestrations of language stir the senses magically.

Dante faced a new linguistic challenge. How to describe a world which cannot easily be put into words? Heaven is a world beyond space and time; a world of light, varied shades of the moon, the pure light of the Empyrean and the fantastical spheres of the heavens. It is all too grand and ineffable for words. Primo Levi lamented the limitations of our language to describe the motions of the planets and the invisible world of the atom. These, Levi believed, were more resistant to our everyday language than the enormity of Auschwitz, where he had been a prisoner. The incredibility of Paradise goes beyond words, therefore Dante invented a verb, *trasumanar*, meaning 'to transcend' or 'transhumanize' beyond the human condition, in order to communicate the difficulty. (The title of the poet and film maker Pier Paolo Pasolini's last verse collection, *Trasumanar e organizzar*, 'Transcend and Organize', published in 1971, honours Dante's neologism.) Apprehension of divine reality necessitates a transcendence of human language and comprehension. Yet Dante's experience of *trasumanar*, of rising above the everyday human, is miraculously accomplished and described in words.

> The blazing of the sunlight seemed to make
> the sky so far enflamed no rain or river
> ever resulted in so broad a lake.
> The newness of the sound and the great light
> which shoots its shafts towards a happy end.

Dante's journey through Paradise will take approximately twenty-four hours. Beatrice remains his 'sweet guide' (*dolce guida)* until the Empyrean, where she is replaced by St Bernard of Clairvaux, the renewer of monasticism in the Western church and a devoted follower of the Virgin Mary. As Dante is guided upwards a measure of his progress is the steadily magnifying beauty of Beatrice: the radiance of her eyes, the radiance of her 'holy smile' (*santo riso*). Sonnets in the *Vita nuova* had conveyed the effect of Beatrice's 'angelic' smile, which consumed the hearts of 'men and angels'; here, her smile is enough to 'make men happy in Hell's fire'. Beatrice has come to represent the light that kindles universal love. (The word *amore,* love, occurs a total of eighty-five times in *Paradiso.*) But love is viewed not as erotic desire but as the desire for the common good, and the greatest good is God. Of course, as Beatrice had told Dante at the end of *Purgatorio,* human love can easily be misdirected by hollow and 'false images of the good' (T. S. Eliot's glittery images of 'Garlic and sapphires in the mud'). But as Beatrice guides Dante up and up into a 'higher blessedness' the poet will know a final stage of contrition and purification.

Accordingly, the words for light steadily multiply through the poem: *luce, sfavilla, scintilla, splendore, fulgore.* (There are approximately seventy occurences of *luce* in *Paradiso.*) The prophet-baptizer St John, patron of Florence, appears before Dante in such a blaze of light that it causes Dante momentarily to go blind. He is like someone who, wishing to see, becomes sightless: '*che, per veder, non vedente diventa*'. Yet his blindness leads not into another dark wood of ignorance, but to an ever-proliferating light and an alignment of Dante's soul with Beatrice's love. The bedazzlement is in the Pauline tradition of a divine revelation that dispels every last trace of sadness and desolating doubt. St Paul's experience on the Damascus road, when he was 'blinded by the light' (as the Bruce Springsteen song has it), is the precedent for Dante's poetic blindness and the inexpressible flash of understanding that follows. Dante has now seen something that is 'not lawful for a man to reveal' – he has seen St John, the precursor of Jesus Christ. St John reassures Dante that Beatrice will be able to restore his extinguished sight (*lo viso spento*).

And, in canto 28, amid a blaze of elevated language and angelic mystery, Beatrice is said to have 'imparadised' Dante's mind (''*mparadisa la mia mente*'). The poet has seen the light and he now *sees* by the light. It is the morning of the thirteenth day of April 1300, the penultimate day of his pilgrimage. Dante now enters the Empyrean. His labours are almost complete and he is about to be shown a redeemed universe. And this universe is also an image of a redeemed love for Beatrice:

> From the first day that I saw her face
> on earth, until this sight, no obstacle
> could prevent me from following her;
> but now I must give up following
> behind her beauty as I write my poem,
> like any artist who has reached his limit.

Beatrice's beauty is now seen at its fullest and most queenly. The occasionally haughty poet has become again almost a child as he trembles at the gaze, at last regained, of his love. The courtly love tradition on which Dante's earliest love poetry was founded returns as Beatrice is pictured as the idea of "Love from a distance" – '*Amor de lonh*' the Provençal Troubadour poets called it. Purged and purified Dante has come out of the depths to contemplate divine infinity. The light pours out of the poet in a heaven which is itself pure light (*pura luce*). The dismal hiss and strife of Hell are no more. In a poetry of strange mesmeric beauty, Beatrice draws Dante into the yellow heart of the white rose of Paradise. Dante achieves here what no poet had attempted (nor has attempted since): the presentation of a world beyond the perception of sense. The light of the Empyrean is an 'intellectual light, full of love', Beatrice explains. It is something we can understand only with our minds. Amid a hum of golden-winged bees she invites the poet to see the blessed systematically arranged and white-robed within the white flower, in the presence of God. The limitless Celestial Rose is formed from a ray of light reflected off the convex surface of the Primum Mobile, the largest and swiftest sphere in Dante's cosmology, from which all movements in the universe derive. For all its standard Arabo-Islamic associations of beauty, perfume and luminousness, the rose-as-heaven is Dante's own invention. He may have had in mind the rose windows of medieval gothic churches.

> Into the yellow of the eternal rose,
> which expands and rises in ranks, and exhales
> fragrance of praise to the Sun that makes perpetual spring,
> Beatrice drew me, silent and wanting to speak,
> and said to me: 'Now see how great it is,
> the congregation of white robes!'

Midway through canto 31 Beatrice leaves Dante; her mission accomplished, she resumes her seat in the heavenly hierarchy, the brightest star of *The Divine Comedy* now pulsing quiet. Dante is 'transhumanized' – transfigured, transubstantiated - into glory; the moon hangs spectral in the radiant heaven; music floats on the air. Here, in the final canto, the word 'light' – *luce* or *lume* – is mentioned ten times. God is light and God is addressed as 'Light Supreme'. And this light, eerily, is a colourless flame that burns in the void without any visible source. Dante's absorption into the divine is complete. Gone is the complicated shame and moral stain of his exile. The canto reaches 'the highest point that poetry has ever reached or ever can reach', T. S. Eliot believed.

Dante is refined out of existence and his spiritual enthronement is achieved.

> But already my desire and my will
> were being turned like a wheel, all at one speed,
>   by the Love which moves the sun and all the stars.

And those are the last lines of Dante Alighieri's *Divine Comedy.*

Rewriting
Holy Writ

A poor translation can resemble the reverse of a tapestry – a 'frayed and ragged version of the original', according to *Don Quixote*'s Miguel de Cervantes. *The Divine Comedy* is a work of such magnitude that, down the centuries, translations have been attempted many times, in particular of the *Inferno*. Among the countless English language versions of that brimstone poem, only a handful have approached the drum-beat rhythm and lyric beauty of the original. The skill required to reproduce the sound and spirit – the *respiro*, breath – of Dante's Tuscan vernacular is considerable.

A special difficulty is Dante's supple triple rhyme known as the *terza rima*. Not a word in his rhyming tercets is unjustified, unintended or extraneous; there are no laxities or verbal redundancies. This allows the translator little room for error. Some have attempted to work within the *terza rima,* others have translated the poem into blank verse, or free verse, prose or rhyming couplets. With a few notable exceptions, the more strenuously original the translation, the less successful it is likely to be. '*Traduttore traditore*' as Italians say. 'The translator is a traitor'.

The Divine Comedy was not rendered into English in complete form until the Romantic period of the early nineteenth century. Before then, we have only extracts, borrowings and adaptations. The first known reference to Dante's work in English occurs within the pages of *The Canterbury Tales* by Geoffrey Chaucer. On two occasions Chaucer travelled to Italy in order to arrange commercial treaties for the English Crown. Before arriving at the Italian seaport of Genoa in 1373 he passed through France, where Italian was known as *la langue de Dante*, 'Dante's tongue'. Dante had been dead for only fifty years, but *The Divine Comedy* was revered in France. (Marguerite de Navarre, sister of the French king Francis I, offered a determinedly mystical response to Dante's masterpiece in her 1548 evangelical poem, *Les Prisons*.) As a controller of customs with business errands to run between London and Italy, and moreover as a vintner's son, Chaucer would have been well-read in Italian and likely to have had connections with Italians (wine merchants among them) resident in London. Both *The Divine Comedy* and commentaries on the work permeated mercantile Italian culture in the fourteenth century. Chaucer may even have been shown the manuscript copy of *The Divine Comedy* made in Genoa in around 1337 – the oldest known copy still in existence. Or perhaps he was introduced to *The Divine Comedy* by Boccaccio, author of the *Decameron* (which Chaucer knew well). Chaucer may have met Boccaccio in Florence in 1373 during his first business mission to Italy (on behalf of Edward III of England). Boccaccio would have been sixty, and Chaucer thirty; since neither man mentions the other, however, their meeting is uncertain.

As far as we know, Chaucer made no direct translation of Dante (though there is the curious reference to Chaucer having composed 'Dante in ynglyssh' by the fifteenth-century monk-poet John Lydgate). Two years after his return to England, around 1375, he began to adapt the grisly Count Ugolino episode from the end of the *Inferno*, renaming Dante's Pisan count Ugolino 'Hugelyn of Pyze'. Chaucer incorporated this story in the Canterbury cycle written some time after 1387, where Hugelyn features as one of several men (Samson, Julius Caesar, Hercules) who, in the Monk's retelling, fall from great prosperity 'into myserie'. Dante's original verse derives from events that the Florentine poet had lived through when he was twenty-three years old. Ugolino de' Gherardeschi, the leader of the Guelf government in Pisa, had traitorously turned Ghibelline but was in turn betrayed by the Pisan Ghibelline leader, Archbishop Ruggieri of Pisa, a man he had trusted. Ugolino was arrested in the winter of 1289 on a charge of treason. Together with two sons and two grandsons he was imprisoned in a tower, the door nailed shut and, on Ruggieri's order, the key thrown away. After eight days all five of the family

overleaf
Ugolino and his sons by the nineteenth-century French painter Charles-Hippolyte-Émile Lecomte-Vernet. At least two of Ugolino's children appear to be unconscious.

were found dead of starvation and thirst. Even in a land inured to human cruelty, people were shocked by the barbarousness of Ugolino's punishment. Where the story appears in *The Canterbury Tales* the tavern host confidently expects to hear a jolly tale from the Monk; instead the Monk relates only a series of tragedies of men brought from high to low estate. Chaucer emphasizes the pathos of the children's fate in the dismal 'Hunger Tower', where Dante does not. (If we are dissatisfied with the Canterbury version, Chaucer tells us, we must read the 'grete poete of Ytalie', a fellow called 'Dant'.) Chaucer's 'veray parfit' Knight afterwards joins in with the host in proclaiming the Monk's story too much for the pilgrims to bear ('good sire, namoore of this!'). Chaucer's literary 'cannibalism' of Dante had upset the pilgrim storytellers.

The dark night-side of Dante's imagination emerges in the Ugolino episode. Dante and Virgil are in the ninth and lowest circle of Hell -- the circle of traitors – where everything is frozen in ice and void of light. The base of Hell is freezing cold because the sinners there have all committed crimes in 'cold blood' and are trapped now like flies in an ice cube. Treachery freezes the soul; so the treacherous are frozen for eternity. Or, as Samuel Beckett put it in *Texts for Nothing* 'Plunged in ice up to the nostrils, the eyelids caked with frozen tears.' In this glacial nadir Dante and his guide stumble on two heads wedged the one above the other in the same ice hole. Count Ugolino is chewing on the neck of the head below his; the head belongs to Archbishop Ruggieri. Ugolino's hunger will never be sated and is unrelieved in its viciousness. The historical question of whether Ugolino actually ate his own children in an attempt to save himself from starvation in February 1289 is insoluble; Dante, on hearing the tale from Ugolino, seems to want us to suspect it. Certainly Ugolino must have committed a crime worse than treason to merit such a *contrapasso;* Lord Byron coined the phrase 'Ugolino hunger' to describe the damned man's supposed cannibalism.

On his return to Italy six years later in 1378–9, again on commercial business for England (this time for Richard II), Chaucer travelled to Padua province where, four years earlier, the poet laureate Francesco Petrarca, or Petrarch, had died at the age of seventy. Petrarch had been introduced to Dante as a child; his own vernacular writings, introspectively focused on his love for a woman called Laura, were influenced by Dante's early lyrics to Beatrice. The contemplative and melancholic aspects of Petrarchism impressed Chaucer. In his *Troilus and Criseyde*, written around 1385 he adapted Petrarch's sonnet 132: 'If it's not love, then what is it I feel?', a question which the British new wave band Wire asked, seven centuries later, in 'Feeling Called Love'. Dante exerted the greater influence than Petrarch, however. Chaucer's unfinished dream-poem *The House of Fame,* probably begun in 1384 (the date is disputed), is thickset with Dantean references (twenty-five, according to one scholar), and the invocation to Mary in 'The Second Nun's Prologue' from *The Canterbury Tales* is based on St Bernard's prayer to the Virgin in canto 33 of *Paradiso*.

Following Chaucer, we hear little of Dante in English for over three and a half centuries. No significant trace of *The Divine Comedy* appears in the work of the Renaissance poets Sidney (though he does mention Dante), Spenser or Wyatt. Dante's demotically colourful Florentine ('farting parts', 'sludge-swallowers') was thought to show a want of manners and decorum. While Renaissance England was not shy of bawdy writing (Shakespeare's sexual puns; the lexically ribald verse of Ben Jonson), in Dante decency was reckoned to have gone by the board. He ran roughshod over neoclassical rules and refinements. He seemed bizarre and Gothic. Elizabethans delighted to read Italian verse, but on the whole they favoured the Latinate refinements of Petrarch over the 'unhonest and filthie talke' of Dante, as the Florentine poet and diplomat Giovanni della Casa put it in 1552. Petrarch, who was seventeen years old when Dante died in 1321, wrote Latin eclogues of decorousness and poise. They were in fact influenced by Dante, but Petrarch never allowed a vulgarism to ruffle their polish. The Bible might make frequent reference to excrement (there are over twenty allusions to *stercus* – 'filth', 'manure' – in the Vulgate or Latin version), but that could not exonerate Dante from what some Elizabethans saw as his coarse language. The cult of Petrarchism in Europe aimed for a poetry purified of low diction and excess. Petrarch regretted that Dante had chosen to write in Florentine rather than Latin; there could be no significant place for vernacular or 'popular' poetry in Petrarch's ideal of restored classical culture. To be a good poet, one had to write in Latin: Dante had failed the test of *latinitas*.

After Petrarch, it was the Venetian poet and future cardinal Pietro Bembo who further undermined Dante's reputation. Bembo, the most influential literary critic of the Italian Renaissance, makes an appearance in Castiglione's 1528 *The Book of the Courtier,* that great Renaissance treatise on how to get on in life (and for a long time much more influential than Machiavelli's *The Prince*). Like Castiglione, Bembo championed the superiority of courtly manners over arms, and insisted upon modesty, kindness and grace of deportment in everyday life. For all his vaunted propriety, however, for sixteen years Bembo had enjoyed an extramarital affair with Lucrezia Borgia, the wife of the Duke of Ferrara and daughter of Pope Alexander VI (of whom Machiavelli wrote approvingly that he 'never did or thought of anything but deceiving people'). From 1506 to 1511, at the height of the affair, Bembo began to write his book about vernacular speech and linguistic usage called *Prose della volgar lingua*. The book acknowledged Dante's stature as a poet but found his style wanting. His occasional 'vulgarity' was bad enough; worse, though, was his confusion of linguistic registers. The words which Dante chose to use ranged from rough (*rozze*), ugly and dirty (*immonde e brute*), and harsh (*durissime*). The book, completed in 1524, unfolds as a conversation between four Renaissance humanist friends as they espouse the aristocratic virtues of grace and balance in writing. Dante's failure to find a vernacular acceptable to polite courtly society was regrettable. If only he had used 'more pleasing and honourable' words, then his 'fame and praise' would be so much greater today. In a famous simile, Bembo compared the language of the *Commedia* to a beautiful field of corn choked with weeds.

Dante's influence remained faint until the early eighteenth century, when the first pre-Romantic glimmerings were felt. Bembo's (or at any rate Bembist) stylistic prohibitions had combined with a strain of virulent anti-Italianate sentiment ('Italianate Englishmen are incarnate devils', proclaimed the Renaissance scholar Roger Ascham) to put Dante out of favour with English culture. In 1719, however, the English painter and art critic Jonathan Richardson provided a spur to the coming English vogue for Dante when, for the first time since Chaucer, he translated the Ugolino canto. The count has been busily 'knawing' at his 'Horrid Food', the nape of the Archbishop's neck, when he looks up and addresses Dante:

> You will compel me to renew my Grief
> Which e'er I speak oppresses my sad Heart;
> But if I Infamy accumulate
> On him whose Head I knaw, I'le not forbear
> To speak tho' Tears flow faster than my Words.

The sublime assurance of these lines shows the influence of Milton, who was among the very few Englishmen to know *The Divine Comedy* intimately. Having studied Italian at St Paul's School in London, Milton spent the summer of 1638 in Dante's birthplace of Tuscany; there he visited the Benedictine monastery of Vallombrosa that would appear in *Paradise Lost*, where fallen angels lie thick as 'autumnal leaves'. Milton read Dante with sympathy and mentions *The Divine Comedy* six times in his *Commonplace Book*. In 1737–8, almost thirty years after Richardson, Thomas Gray rendered the Ugolino episode into poetry no less sublime; in Ugolino's speech Gray brings out the clammy hideousness of the prison and the cruelty of 'Pisa's perfidious prelate' Ruggieri.

> I heard the dreadful clank of bars
> And fastening of bolts. Then on my children's eyes
> Speechless my sight I fixed, nor wept, for all
> Within was stone

Gray belonged to the generation of young Englishmen who had discovered Dante through the Grand Tour. Usually the tour culminated in Naples, ragamuffin capital of the Italian south where Vesuvius offered a visual education in the grand style. Some Grand Tourists, among them Lord Byron, got as far as Greece; but Italy was coveted as the glittering birthplace of the Renaissance. Most commentators date the birth of the Renaissance to 1492, when Lucrezia Borgia's father Rodrigo Borgia became Pope Alexander VI, and Columbus encountered America. Lucrezia herself, a radiant symbol of the new, sexually confident Renaissance woman, was not the fiend history made her out to be. Her ethereal blonde looks so captivated Lord Byron that, in 1816, he stole a strand of her hair from a cabinet in the Ambrosiana library in Milan (presumably when the curator's back was turned). Her love letters to Pietro Bembo moved Byron almost to tears: 'The prettiest love letters in the world', he called them.

In Britain, the Italian peninsula was considered a civilizing influence. 'A man who has not been to Italy', Samuel Johnson observed in 1776, 'is always conscious of an inferiority.' The Cambridge-educated Gray embarked on his Grand Tour in 1739–41; accompanied by his friend the Gothic novelist Horace Walpole (who, incidentally, disliked Dante, calling him 'absurd, extravagant, disgusting', even, bizarrely, 'a Methodist parson in

Bedlam'), Gray went about with a *cicerone* or scholarly guide. It is fair to suppose that Gray carried his copy of the five-volume *Opere* of Dante, published in Venice in 1578. Rome displayed to Gray and Walpole a civilization in ruins. They visited the Colosseum, the Capitol, Palazzo Pamphilj and, further south, Herculaneum. Much of Herculaneum and neighbouring Pompeii had yet to be excavated: shops, brothels, inns and stables were uncovered by the Neapolitan authorities seven years later in 1748. A visit to at least one of the ash-solidified sites was reckoned essential for the Grand Tourist if he (usually he) was to demonstrate a classical education acquired abroad. Ten years later, in 1750, Gray completed his 'Elegy Written in a Country Churchyard', which, he said, was indebted to Dante's *Purgatorio* for its autumnal musings and melancholy.

The first English translation of the entire *Divine Comedy* did not appear until 1802. Reverend Henry Boyd, an Irish cleric born in County Antrim in 1750, translated Ariosto and Petrarch before embarking on Dante. Boyd's was a pioneering version, which introduced Dante to many English readers (among them the artists Henry Fuseli and John Flaxman). On occasion, Boyd's tendency to elaborate took him far from the original. The *aguglia* ('eagle') of canto 9 *Purgatorio* becomes 'plumy Ranger of th' OLYMPIAN throne', which is extravagant. In Boyd, the 'gloomy and romantic' Dante (as the cleric described him) acquires a solemnity and sublimity that, again, echoes Milton:

> AURORA, stealing from her Consort's arms,
> Shew'd in the glimmer'ing East her rising charms;
> The Stars, that form'd the Scorpion's radiant train,
> Gemm'd her pale brow...

Boyd does not so much keep faith with the original as promote an idea of translation as embellishment. His version, first published in Dublin in 1785, contains allusions to Mount Etna and other sights in Italy not found in Dante; most likely Boyd had read of them in accounts of the Grand Tour. Dante was viewed by Boyd, and generally by eighteenth-century England, as either a Promethean poet of melancholy glooms – all fire and smoke – or as a sternly moralizing Christian who fathomed potholes of human sin.

Recast by Boyd and other reverends as Christian hymnology, *The Divine Comedy* became the most serious of poems, its greatness celebrated in Bible classes across the land. Civil servants, bankers, politicians, barristers, many of them hobbyists (among them, in the Victorian age, the chancellor of the exchequer William Gladstone) tried their hand at Dante. Few of these attempts were published; and very few translators took on all three books. Twelve years after Boyd, however, in a foretaste of British Dante-mania, the Reverend Henry Francis Cary began to translate the trilogy into Miltonic blank verse. Issued in 1814 at Cary's own expense, *The Vision; or, Hell, Purgatory and Paradise, of Dante Alighieri* is the first serious translation of all the parts of Dante's poem in English. (*The Vision* was a title that Cary found 'more comfortable to the genius of our language than that of *The Divine Comedy*.) Unfortunately the print was microscopic and there were scant footnotes. *The Vision* attracted just two reviews – one favourable, one contemptuous – and absolutely no sales. All that changed when Samuel Taylor Coleridge praised the translation in a lecture he gave on Dante four years later, in 1818. Coleridge had wished to read Dante in the original Italian ever since he toured Italy in 1804 wearing a pair of 'green solar spectacles'. The 'Gentleman-poet and Philosopher-in-a-mist' (as Coleridge described himself) was in many ways Dante's ideal advocate. A perfect Proteus, he could discourse on fossilism, metallurgy, fell walking and *The Divine Comedy* in a torrent of donnish table talk. The faculty of wonder in Coleridge – his open-mouthed appreciation of beauty – was to the fore in the lecture he delivered on Dante at the Philosophical Society of London. Dante's poem, Coleridge judged, was a 'proto-Romantic epic' of 'endless subtle beauties', as well as endless horror. Thanks to Coleridge, the first edition of *The Vision* sold out and appreciative reviews began to appear in the *Edinburgh Review*, *Quarterly Review* and other august journals. It was agreed: Cary had outstripped all his predecessors. His burial place in Westminster Abbey is under a stone marked 'THE TRANSLATOR OF DANTE'. The emphatic definite article is deserved; Cary's was – and remains – a superlative Dante.

As men of the cloth, the reverends Boyd and Cary struggled in particular with canto 21 of the *Inferno* where Barbariccia (Curly-Beard) makes a 'trumpet' of his backside and breaks wind musically. The farts are decorously rendered by Boyd as 'loud Aeolian fifes', after the ancient Greek god of wind, while Cary blushingly settled for a 'sound obscene' – an effect rather like that of drinking flat champagne. Another English clergyman, E. H. Plumptre, Dean of Wells in Somerset, spent twenty years poring over Dante before his late Victorian-era *Commedia and Canzoniere* appeared with various of Dante's other poems in a single volume in 1887. Plumptre's timid literalisms and expurgations were no less marked than those of Boyd and Cary. Barbariccia's foul bum-belches become 'trumpet notes' that from his 'back parts did breathe'. This is misleadingly tame. What Cary translates as 'back parts' is bare *cul* in the Italian original, as in the contemporary Italian *culo*, or arse. Dante's scatology is never mealy-mouthed.

John Keats first read Dante in the 1814 three-volume Cary, which he took with him on his 1818 walking tour of the Lake District and Scotland. To his brother George he had written that it was 'well worth the while' to learn Italian in order to read the original, which he did, presumably using Cary as a crib. Most of the English Romantic poets came to Dante through Cary. His translation saw a surge of interest in touring Italy for its art and classical antiquity. The Grand Tour, begun in the mid-seventeenth century, would continue until the advent of rail transport in the 1840s. For the consumptive Keats, the idea of the warm south provided a hoped-for balm to the deadly tubercle bacillus. Eventually Keats travelled to Rome. Shelley, too, saw Italy as a promise of intoxicating self-forgetfulness. In his 1821 essay *A Defence of Poetry* Shelley exalts Dante's verse as a 'bridge thrown over the stream of time, which unites the modern and ancient world'.

With the Romantics, the Paolo and Francesca episode from canto 5 of the *Inferno* superseded the Ugolino episode in popularity; perhaps fortunately so, for as John Ruskin later lamented, the Ugolino episode 'was the only bit of Dante that English people have ever read.' Canto 5 is where Dante encounters for the first time souls who have not repented. The adulterous lovers Paolo Malatesta and Francesca da Rimini are found writhing without hope in a black whirlpool. Having died of lust they are allowed to speak to Dante for a few minutes. Francesca explains how love has been her undoing; she and her brother-in-law Paolo had exchanged their first kiss on reading the story of Lancelot's passion for Guinevere. All this happened just a few years before the date of Dante's journey. It raises the question of what distinguishes this love from Dante's love for Beatrice. How close to damnation Dante might have come is perhaps why he faints. ('I swoon'd, as if by death I had been smote', Lord Byron translated the canto in 1820, 'And fell down even as a dead body falls.') Before swooning to the ground he allows Francesca one of the greatest lines in the poem: '*Nessun maggiore dolore che ricordarsi del tempo felice nella miséra*' ('There is no greater pain, than to remember, in our present grief, past happiness'); a line reiterated by a gondolier in Rossini's opera *Otello* and by Boccaccio in the introduction to his poem *Il filostrato* (*The Love Struck*).

Why this story so appealed to the Romantic poets is not hard to understand. Married to an unattractive, deformed older man, Gianciotto Malatesta, Francesca could not resist kissing the beautiful Paolo, her husband's brother. (Rodin's sculpture 'The Kiss' was intended to represent the Italian lovers in their unwitnessed ecstasy.) For ten years Francesca remained Paolo's secret lover until her husband Gianciotto discovered the affair and ran them both through with a sword. Now the lovers are condemned to the second circle of Hell reserved for those overcome by lust. Adultery, near-incest (the lovers are brother and sister-in-law) and murder: this is not a simple story of sin in relation to desire, but of a sin that undermines the patrician order of Florence. It is also a true story. Francesca's lover Paolo had been appointed the Florence *capitano del popolo* ('captain of the people') in February 1282, when the sixteen-year-old Dante may have met him; only a few years after his and Francesca's murder in 1285, Francesca's father was made *podestà* (a high-ranking administrator) of Florence. Beneath their political power the family was mired in scandal.

Keats, who wrote so hauntingly of life's uncertainty and of his own consumptive state, dreamed one night that he was in Francesca's alluring presence. 'The dream was one of the most delightful enjoyments I ever had in my life', he wrote to his brother George and sister-in-law Georgina in 1819; locked in a shuddering drawn-out kiss with Francesca he floated like a ghost in the dream's 'whirling atmosphere'. On waking Keats resolved to describe the dream in a sonnet; the erotic charge is unmistakable:

Pale were the sweet lips I saw
Pale were the lips I kiss'd and fair the form
I floated with about that melancholy storm –

As Dante had inspired Chaucer to recast Ugolino in 'The Monk's Tale', so Dante inspired the English Romantics to attempt their versions of tales from *The Divine Comedy*. Their interest in Dante was less scholarly than enthusiastic, but it attested to

overleaf William Blake, *The Lovers' Whirlwind*. Francesca da Rimini
and Paolo Malatesta float above Dante in a halo-like cloud.
At the bottom of the watercolour Blake has written: 'HELL. Canto 5'.

HELL Canto 5

Dante's growing popular readership in England. In 1816, Keats's friend Leigh Hunt published his version of canto 5 in the long poem *The Story of Rimini*, where Francesca and Paolo (misspelled or Anglicized by Hunt as 'Paulo') are transformed into Romantic archetypes of doomed love. Leigh Hunt amplifies the sixty or so lines in Dante to an impressive 1,706: mere narrative hints in the *Inferno* become full-blown episodes. The poem opens in medieval Ravenna one morning in the spring of 1275. Crowds are gathered, among them the 'knightly' *dolce stil novo* poet Guido Cavalcanti. After the marriage vows between Francesca and Gianciotto, 'like peaches on a tree', Paulo and Francesca are seen pressed together in a tender fluttering of hearts. Gramsci spoke of their 'spiritual grace'; they are compared to a pair of doves as they fly towards Dante and Virgil: their love was more than carnal. Leigh Hunt finally published his own, magnificent translation of canto 5 in 1846, at the age of sixty-two, by which time the greatest poet-physician in the English language, John Keats, had been dead for a quarter of a century.

In time, Dante's darkness attenuated into something more palatable. Thomas Love Peacock's novella *Headlong Hall*, published in the same year as Leigh Hunt's *The Story of Rimini*, (1816), has a Coleridge-like Mr Cornelius Chromatic perform an after-dinner Dante entertainment. With the help of his two daughters he regales Squire Harry Headlong and his assembled guests with an unwittingly dire imitation of *Purgatorio* canto 8 where a penitent Christian renders before God an evening hymn – a Te lucis ante. The lines, intended to capture the romance of sunset, merely suggest bardic pretension, and out-purple anything by Dante's worst translators:

> Grey Twilight her shadowy hill,
> Discolours Nature's vernal bloom,
> And sheds on grove, and field, and rill,
> One placid tint of deepening gloom.

Peacock's novella is an indication of how Dante had become almost a parlour entertainment in England. Between 1825 and 1914 there were more than twenty musical operas based on the Paolo and Francesca story, some of them comic, but most of them melodramas in a dark spirit of Byronism, black secrecy and sex.

After Keats died in Rome in 1821, his tubercular expectorations having turned 'black and thick in the extreme', it was left to Shelley to carry the English flame for Dante.

Shelley's translations of Dante's verse were incomplete at his death in 1822, at the age of only twenty-eight. Almost alone among the Romantics Shelley preferred *Purgatorio* and *Paradiso* to the *Inferno*, always stressing 'the exquisite tenderness & sensibility & ideal beauty, in which Dante excelled all poets except Shakspeare.' Shelley's was a very different Dante to Byron's Promethean figure. According to Shelley, Dante 'understood the secret things of love'; Shelley considered *Paradiso* a 'perpetual hymn of everlasting love' waiting to be kindled into English.

He thought highly of Cary's translation, but was less impressed by Cary's refusal (or inability) to work within the Dantescan *terza rima*. Shelley considered it 'an essential justice to an author, to render him in the same form.' The *terza rima* was a form to which Shelley would often return in his own poetry (most wonderfully, in 'Ode to the West Wind' and 'Triumph of Life', in which T. S. Eliot rightly saw 'some of the greatest and most Dantesque lines in English'). Other Romantic poets, among them Byron and Leigh Hunt, considered Dante's triple rhyme a stimulus rather than a deterrent, and produced translations of a taut cadence and enduring vigour – though none could approach Shelley for his zealous advocacy of the Italian tercet. Completed in 1820, his translation of canto 28 of *Purgatorio* is magnificent. Dante has journeyed through a Hell of maimed, halt and twisted sinners to the 'divine forest' of the Earthly Paradise: the scene is suffused with a lambent other-worldly glow. Birds chirrup –

already Dante has arrived at a condition of the blessed:

> Yet were they not so shaken from their rest
> But that the birds, perched on the utmost spray,
> Incessantly renewing their blithe quest
>
> With perfect joy received the early day
> Singing within the glancing leaves, whose sound
> Kept one low burthen to their roundelay...

Shelley's acquaintance with Dante deepened in 1818, when, for the first (and, it turned out, only) time he visited Italy and stayed there for four years. In April he wrote to Thomas Love Peacock that he had been reading *The Divine Comedy* in a tenebrous corner of Milan Cathedral. By the time Shelley arrived at Naples in November, seven months later, he was quite estranged from his wife Mary. His low mood was aggravated by the birth of the couples' mysterious 'Neapolitan charge' Elena Adelaide. Nobody has yet been able to identify Elena's parents; she was falsely registered as the child of Mary and Percy Bysshe Shelley at the Naples orphanage of Santa Maria dell'Annunziata. Most likely she was the child of one of Shelley's lovers, who may or may not have tried to seek him out in Italy. Naples had its incidental pleasures. The *pensione* where Shelley was staying with Mary at 250 Riviera di Chaia was a half-hour walk from Virgil's columbarium tomb, originally shaded by a giant bay tree that was said to have withered in 1321 at the moment of Dante's death. Elena Adelaide herself died in Naples at the age of two.

When, in 1822, Shelley drowned while sailing in the Gulf of La Spezia, a volume of Keats was found in his pocket. His premature end could not have been more poetic. His ashes were buried in Rome in the same cemetery as Keats, who had died a year earlier in rooms overlooking the Spanish Steps. During his time in Italy, Shelley had read at least two cantos of *Purgatorio* every day to his wife Mary, possibly in hope of repairing their marriage.

Fifteen years after the deaths of Keats and Shelley, Queen Victoria ascended the throne. The year was 1837. Europe was a decade away from its 1848 'Year of Revolutions', when Dante (according to one biographer, 'the most Italian poet there ever was') would be adopted as the embodiment of nationalist *italianità* – 'Italian-ness'. Already in 1821 Lord Byron had hailed Dante as the prophet of future Italian unity in his poem, 'Prophecy of Dante', where Dante foretells the fortunes of 'Italia' in the centuries following his death. The Tuscan tongue will be elevated over Latin; the syntax of *The Divine Comedy* will shape a new national language of Italy; and Italy will emerge as 'Europe's nightingale of song'.

*

In the mid-nineteenth century revolutions and nationalist up-risings were burning like fires across Europe. Elizabeth Barrett Browning declared that Dante would have thrilled 'with ecstasy' had he known of the Liberal demonstrations that convulsed Florence in 1848. On the Italian peninsula, the Risorgimento or 'resurgence' under Giuseppe Garibaldi, Camillo Benso, count of Cavour, and Giuseppe Mazzini would liberate most of the Italian peoples from their abhorred Habsburg and Bourbon rulers. Appropriately, lines from *The Divine Comedy* were taken up as Risorgimento hymns:

> O abject Italy, O seat of sorrow,
> Vessel without a pilot in a storm,
> Not queen of provinces, but a bordello!

Italian unification was declared by parliament in the northern Italian city of Turin in 1861. The idealists and patriots who struggled for independence were mostly from the north;

overleaf
The Funeral of Shelley by Louis Edouard Fournier, 1889.
On the bleak, windswept beach in La Spezia the poet's widow
Mary kneels in sorrow; Lord Byron is gazing out to sea.

Louis-Edouard Fournier
1889

annexation with the impoverished south was tantamount (in the words of one Turinese grandee) to 'getting into bed with a smallpox victim'. So Turin – not Rome – became the first capital of united Italy. The northern city's arcaded piazzas and geometric avenues were reckoned a salubrious alternative to Rome's dark, malarial backstreets. Full political unification was not achieved until Rome and a remainder of the Papal States joined the Kingdom of Italy in 1870. The Risorgimento saw every Italian town erect a statue of Dante in a Piazza Dante created for the occasion. Dante had long dreamed of a united Italy (though not a self-governing one); now, five centuries on, it seemed that his vision was at last realized. The official language adopted by the new nation state of Italy was a literary language based on Dante's Florentine. It was spoken mostly by the upper and mercantile classes of Tuscany; more than ninety per cent of Italians continued to speak not Italian, but a regional dialect. Italy's dialects were (indeed still are) an amalgam of Latin and languages spoken by the bewildering number of ethnicities that have populated the peninsula and, down the centuries, formed a loose-knit Italic kin of Albanians, Normans, Saracens, Greeks and Germanic *longobardi* ('long beards', later Lombards). The literary Italian 'invented' by Dante would soon become the language of the new Italian nation, the contemporary language of schools, universities, professionals and teachers. The Victorian poets Algernon Swinburne and the laureate Alfred Tennyson joined Elizabeth Barrett Browning in their reverence of Dante as a visionary forebear of Italian unification. By the mid-nineteenth century the Florentine poet had become a bestselling author; Staffordshire Dante figurines were sold in their thousands.

Crowds flocked to greet Garibaldi when he visited London in 1864; a new football club, Nottingham Forest, adopted Garibaldi-red as its colour. The Italian patriot 'received an address and gifts of swords and flags from the Italian Committee, and spoke forcefully before over 20,000 people'. Garibaldi called on Tennyson at his summer retreat on the Isle of Wight; the municipality of Florence had commissioned Tennyson to write a poem to honour the 600th anniversary of Dante's birth in 1865 ('King, that has reigned six hundred years'). Garibaldi was not the only Italian nationalist to use Dante's romantic image as leverage for the Risorgimento. Another was the visionary Genoan journalist and pamphleteer Giuseppe Mazzini, who was to inspire two generations of radical liberals and democrats across Europe. Having been denounced by the Vatican as an agent of Satan, Mazzini was exiled to London in 1837, a decade before Marx and Engels settled in the teeming metropolis. In London he moved from one shabby boarding house to another, keeping the curtains permanently drawn for fear of detection. His writings, running to sixty-four volumes of letters and thirty essay collections, mingled a Risorgimento romanticism with a hard-nosed political exigency. Most of Mazzini's writing was banned by the Italian authorities, including even his edition of the Italian Romantic poet Ugo Foscolo's (unfinished) commentary on *La divina commedia,* published in four volumes in London in 1842–3 by the Piedmontese bookseller Pietro Rolandi. Foscolo, himself a patriot exiled to London, was among the first to popularize Dante among English Victorian readers. Rolandi's bookshop, situated on the outskirts of Soho at 20 Berners Street, was frequented by, among others, the Scottish historian Thomas Carlyle and the British Museum Library director Antonio Panizzi (who was under sentence of death in his native Italy for revolutionary activities). Rolandi's Libreria Italiana was intermittently placed under foreign surveillance; Rolandi himself had been vilified and detained during his visit to Italy in 1842 on a mission to distribute Foscolo's Dante in the Mazzini edition. The brown paper-wrapped volumes were removed from Rolandi's person and burned. The bookseller returned to London relieved to be alive. 'Rolandi is like Dante's shipwreck survivor, who "turns and looks back at the deep he has escaped",' Mazzini wrote in 1843, quoting from canto 1 of the *Inferno* (*si volge all'acqua perigliosa e guata*).

Mazzini's first Dante essay, published in 1841, was addressed to 'Italian workers'. Mazzini was a rare Risorgimentist who cared at all for the poor. That same year, with an eye to ameliorating child vagrancy in Victorian London, Mazzini opened a free school in Hatton Garden for Italian street musicians, trinket sellers and other juveniles. The school's in-house journal, *Il Pellegrino* ('The Pilgrim'), a sort of nineteenth-century *Look and Learn,* offered history lessons on illustrious Italians, among them Dante, Christopher Columbus and Leonardo da Vinci. Dante was exalted as a harbinger of 'free nationality' for a new age of liberty; he was 'neither a Catholic nor a Guelf, nor a Ghibelline; he was a Christian and an Italian', Mazzini insisted.

Across the Atlantic, meanwhile, Dante's great champion was the American poet Henry Longfellow who, for all the flowery Victorian idiom of his verse, was attuned to Dante's rhyme-rich Tuscan in a way that few translators have been before or since. Longfellow's *Divine Comedy,* issued in 1855–7, was the first complete and, in many respects, still the best American-English version of the poem. Longfellow was a founder member of the Boston-based Dante Club, whose Italophile men of letters (among them the Harvard scholars James Russell Lowell and Oliver Wendell Holmes) hoped to introduce Dante's poem to a wider New England readership, and in the process fire Boston Brahmins with a sense of moral uplift. From their Puritan forefathers the New England Dantists had inherited a distaste for 'Romanism' and the Pre-Reformation age of Catholic saints and miracles. Yet many were secretly sympathetic to the great art and music inspired by the Church of Rome, and acknowledged that Dante, Raphael, Michelangelo, Pascal and Descartes had all been Catholic. Often their responses to Dante betrayed simultaneously a fear of papist 'corruption' and a hunger for papist 'communion',

Plaster cast of Dante taken shortly after his death in Ravenna in 1321. Political exile may account for the death mask's sad aspect.

The Divine Comedy combining in their minds the simplicity of the meeting house and the baroque splendour of St Peter's.

The Dante Club met with some opposition from the jingoistic Harvard Corporation, who feared that an English Dante translation might introduce elements of papist 'immorality' into the Yankee heartlands. Longfellow, at heart a crypto Catholic, did not see Dante as a Protestant spirit set against the Church of Rome; papal purple was not for him a sign of dangerous recusancy. Matthew Pearl, in his pastiche nineteenth-century whodunit, *The Dante Club,* published in 2004, relates how a Boston serial killer attempts to discredit the 'Romish' Longfellow and his Brahmin 'dantistas' by inflicting gruesome punishments from the *Inferno* on his victims. (A Unitarian minister is burned alive in a cesspit; a high court judge is found to be crawling with maggots.) America, soon to be torn apart in the Civil War, was fearful of unknown 'foreign influences'. In Victorian England, under the guidance of Cardinals John Henry Newman and Henry Edward Manning, Catholicism survived against the odds; but America, slower to embrace the 'old religion', took time to absorb Dante's Catholic spirit.

Those who know *The Divine Comedy* from the three-volume Penguin Classic published between 1949 and 1962 are often surprised to find that it was translated by the same Dorothy L. Sayers ('Wee Dolly Sayers', T. S. Eliot called her) who gave us Lord Peter Wimsey. Sayers's dandified detective owns a private Dante collection which, we read in *Whose Body?,* 'includes, besides the famous Aldine octavo of 1502, the Naples folio of 1477.' Such bibliographic pedantry squares with Sayers's own linguistic punctilio. She worked devotedly on her Dante translation for the last thirteen years of her life. By paring back the existing Victorian distortions and literalisms, she arrived at a scholarly rehabilitation of the original, which, in spite of the odd 'forsooth' of Victorian knightly romanticism, approximated happily enough to the rough grain of Dante's speech. Sayers is the only woman to have achieved recognition as a Dante translator; to date, sales of her Penguin Classic (which she dedicated to the Anglican-mystic critic Charles Williams) exceed those of all other versions combined (with the exception perhaps of Cary's, which, curiously, provided the text for the Eternal Kool Project's 2005 *Inferno Rap,* a hip-hop Dante). When Sayers died in 1957, at the age of sixty-four, she was still at work on 'Paradise'. This canticle was completed by her friend Barbara Reynolds, a renowned Dante scholar, but it was Sayers who led thousands of new readers to the work. Of course, no Penguin translation can last for ever. Sayers's has now been superseded by Robin Kirkpatrick's, whose *The Divine Comedy,* published in 2012, jettisoned *terza rima* for unrhymed verse.

Among other recent translations, Steve Ellis's *Hell* (1994) is distinguished by its rude and racy idiom: 'tart', 'bonce', 'shite'. The free verse translation draws on words and speech patterns of the translator's native Yorkshire – fittingly so, given the Florentine dimension, the *italianità fiorentina* of the original. Northern-sounding words ('beck', 'mire', 'gutted', 'lads') accord well with Florentine *volgare.* Indeed, demotic vulgarisms such as 'crap like this' for *simile lordura* or 'dire smell' for *tristo fiato* serve to meld medieval Florence with modern Yorkshire. Strikingly, the *doloroso ospizio* of canto 5 is rendered by Ellis as 'hopeless hotel', which Sayers and others have more conventionally translated as a medieval 'house of pain', after a medieval lazar house for lepers or an almshouse. Ellis's 'hotel' for '*ospizio*' not only connotes medieval hospitality; it admirably catches Dante's ironic use of the term in the context of Hell: 'hotel' is more usually a place of refuge. In a 1994 newspaper review of *Hell* I queried Ellis's rendering of the poem's opening line: 'trek' for *cammin* had seemed to me misguided:

> Halfway through our trek in life
> I found myself in this dark wood

The word 'trek', Afrikaans for 'travel by ox-wagon', conjures an image of hill-hiker shoes or sports shops; instead we should enter the poem in a magical way. Ellis wrote back to express his disappointment at my objection to the word:

> With an opening as well-worn as Dante's, it seemed important to make a bid straight away for the kind of translation I wanted, one condensed and colloquial. 'Trek' also suggests something dour and fatiguing; it's a word York City supporters might use to describe a trip to Crewe, or my ageing mother for her journey to the local shops, and it's surely sufficiently naturalized into English to evoke no longer Afrikaans ox wagons.

Ellis's letter concluded:

> *I've floated 'trek' up and down the country in talking about the translation in the last year, and a majority of my audience seem to have favoured it; at any rate, it provoked a response. Can anyone feel aroused, for or against, by the line Mr Thomson would put in its place, Longfellow's* 'Midway upon the journey of our life'?

Dante himself thought translation to be impossible: 'nothing which is bound together in harmonious form by musical ligatures', he wrote in his philosophical treatise, the *Convivio*, 'can possibly be translated from one language into another without losing entirely its sweetness and harmony'. However, first lines are important – and none more so than *The Divine Comedy*'s. Ellis's 'trek' is preferable to Elizabeth Barrett Browning's 'road of life':

> All in the middle of the road of life
> I stood bewildered in a dusky wood

Barrett Browning's 'middle of the road', with its modern connotations of 'safe', 'beige', 'unadventurous' or 'middle of the road' feels too homely. Now consider William Hayley's early nineteenth-century version, which introduces the word 'mortal':

> In the mid season of this mortal strife,
> I found myself within a gloomy grove

As a chaplain, Hayley wished to show that the meaning of life is everywhere connected to what it means to die: Dante as memento mori. Henry Cary, an archdeacon's grandson, made the same notable addition:

> In the midway of our mortal life,
> I found myself in a gloomy wood, astray

Religious men, Hayley and Cary saw death as a release from earthly cares – a reminder that the undertaker, whatever the innovations of medicine, awaits us all. Their inclusion of 'mortal' is understandable, therefore, but it compromises the elegance of Dante's original.

None of these opening lines by Ellis, Barrett Browning, Hayley and Cary is bad – each one exhibits craft and adequate accuracy – but they are not quite Dante. Of the forty-seven English language versions of *The Divine Comedy* currently held at the British Library, not one can decide on how best to render the '*selva oscura*' of the famous opening canto. Some refer to the wood as 'dusky' or 'darksome', others 'drear', or 'darkling' or 'darkened'. In a sense, Dante must remain the great un-translatable; some insurmountable cross-cultural divide means that the peculiar savour of his work cannot easily be reinvented through the words of others. Here, in all its strange glory, is the original:

> Nel mezzo del cammin di nostra vita
> mi ritrovai per una selva oscura
> ché la diritta via era smarrita.

Like Sayers before him, the Belfast poet Ciaran Carson worked within Dante's *terza rima* for his wonderfully different version of 'The Inferno' published in 2002. By inserting archaisms from eighteenth-century Irish ballads, Carson restored a vocal music to the canticle. William Morris had done something similar with Homer, converting the *Odyssey* into a weird ballad-speak, as if the poem had descended from the smoky throne rooms of northern Europe. Common insults – 'let him have it up the bum!', 'up yours', 'you little squit' – bring Carson's translation closer to the coarse grain of Chaucer's *Canterbury Tales*. At other times, hints of American ('palooka', 'spiel', 'Vamoose') suggest the off-Broadway street slang of Damon Runyon. Carson's translation has a political edge. His rendering of the 'vendetta-stricken' families and rival clans of 1300s Florence carries a deliberate echo of the civic strife and political divisions within North Belfast. Hell itself has 'borders' and 'precincts'; of his 'divided city' Dante asks: 'Is there one just man in it? Or are they all sectarians?' Few assassinations or ambushes or vendettas convulsed Belfast while Carson was at work on his translation, but the politically loaded word 'sectarian' serves to propel 'The Inferno' into a present-day politics of compromise, Orange parades, paramilitary zealots, 'Loyalist enclaves', 'no-go zones', Ulster Freedom Fighters, and Northern Irish troubles generally. A British army helicopter was occasionally to be heard clattering and whirring overhead near the old Belfast Waterworks where Carson then lived.

Other contemporary translations have been no less inventive. Philip Terry's satirical *Dante's Inferno,* published in 2014, is set on the University of Essex campus, renowned once for its far-left politics. Virgil's place is taken by Ted Berrigan, the 1960s New York School poet who served in Korea as a soldier and died young of alcohol and drugs. An affable presence, Berrigan guides the translator Terry through the 'doleful campus' with its clutter of funding bodies, health and safety signs and students patrolling the sunless corridors. A wide range of characters and modern reference from Paris Hilton to Edward Scissorhands adds new vigour to Dante's *Inferno.* The Reverend Ian Paisley, the loyalist politician who, we read, 'tore everything apart with schism', stands in for the Prophet Muhammad in canto 28, while the IRA hunger striker Bobby Sands is seen to chew on the head of Margaret Thatcher. Dante's *rozzore* (roughness) comes through in Terry's deployment of scatology and pop vernacular (Berrigan's eyes are long dead 'through speed and booze'). Corrupted financiers and other arch-felons responsible for the 2008 credit crunch – convicted 'shysters' all – are subjected to endless misery and woe. Taking proper measure of the 2008 financial enormities Berrigan quotes from the Bob Dylan song 'Masters of War': 'All the money you made will never buy back your soul'.

In 2006 the poet and playwright Sean O'Brien, also Belfast-born, offered a verse translation of *Hell* with a comparable surfeit of slang ('dishevelled, shitty hag' for *sozza e scapigliata fante*; 'hot sauce' for *pungenti salse*). Few twenty-first-century translators have been brave enough to take on *Purgatorio* and *Paradiso* as well as the *Inferno*, though the Australian-born polymath Clive James is an exception. In 2013, James published his version of the entire poem with the name CLIVE JAMES blown up to the size of Dante's on the cover. Unlike Sayers and Carson, James chose not to work within Dante's tercets; instead, he smoothly rendered the interlocking three-line chains into rhymed quatrains. Shakespeare wrote in quatrains, but they are not in the end sympathetic to Dante's Trinitarian theology. By attempting *terza rima,* Carson and Sayers kept faith with a Dantescan spirit of trinity as mirrored in the poem's overall tripartite design; James is unable, or does not want to do this.

Like many translators, James fills out his *Divine Comedy* with antiquarianisms ('whereat', 'doth', 'aught else', 'yonder'), which give the impression that Dante wrote in an Italian that sounded two centuries old to his first readers, when he really did not. In this version, worn phrases cling to the dense pentameter lines ('cheek by jowl', 'dubious privilege', 'vaulting pride'); but rather than work with the grain of Dante's speech, these serve to recall the brilliant tongue of James the journalist and television personality. In his introduction, James upbraids Sayers for perceived deficiencies in her Penguin Classic: Sayers had 'simultaneously loaded her text with cliché and pumped it full of wind.' Yet James is no less guilty of expanding the poem. In lieu of footnotes he interpolates explanatory material not found in the original. (Minos is a 'connoisseur of turpitude'; the *dolce stil novo* poet Forese Donati is Dante's 'fellow sonneteer'.) Dante never stoops to this sort of explication. Cumulatively, James's additions make for a *Divine Comedy* a third longer than the original. This is all the more unfortunate in a writer such as Dante, for whom accuracy, precision and concision were sovereign virtues.

One cannot discuss Dante translations into English without turning to T. S. Eliot, who hovers like an Anglo-Catholic atmosphere over all modern versions of *The Divine Comedy*. In Eliot's austere view, Dante was the highest expression of Christian civilization; his medieval trilogy encouraged the Missouri-born poet in his conviction that modern man was spiritually shipwrecked, and served to fortify his High Anglican politics of social conformity. Beneath Eliot's fine yacht-club manners and dandified dress sense was a hesitant and tormented poet unable to 'seize the day' and live life to the full. As a young man he had enjoyed listening to jazz on a wind-up gramophone, but was inhibited by an extreme sexual timorousness. Soon after his marriage in 1915, his wife Vivienne Haigh-Wood started to behave wildly, taking up with the philosopher Bertrand Russell and (it was maliciously put about) others too. Eliot seems not to have retaliated with any infidelities of his own, but in time, Vivienne's mental disarray became entangled with his. In 1921, a nerve specialist advised Eliot to quit his job in Lloyds Bank and take the sea air at Margate. From out of his emotional turbulence came *The Waste Land,* whose imagery of drowning men, doleful shades, sooty London streets and perfunctory sex in sleazy digs suggested a cramped and very buttoned-up poet. 'I had not thought death had undone so many', we read of those London rush-hour commuters in 'The Burial of the Dead' – words that Eliot lifted from line 57, canto 3 of the *Inferno*, though Shelley's short poem 'Hell' may have been a subliminal (and, to my knowledge, curiously unremarked) influence.

> Hell is a city much like London –
> A populous and a smoky city;
> There are all sorts of people undone,
> And there is little or no fun done;
> Small justice shown, and still less pity.

In another clear imitation of Dante, Eliot attempted triple rhyme in 'Little Gidding', the fourth and final poem of *Four Quartets*. His first book of poems, *Prufrock and Other Observations,* carries an epigraph from Dante, as does the first poem in that book, 'The Love Song of J. Alfred Prufrock'. There are more references to Dante in Eliot's *Selected Essays* than to any other writer apart from Shakespeare. Eliot revered Dante as (in Seamus Heaney's phrase) the 'aquiline patron of international Modernism'. He remained wary of 'translationese', however, and avoided translations of Dante that generally appeared to be deficient in fluency or elegance. Instead, he sampled and stole from Dante. Much more than a dictionary is required to do Dante justice; Eliot believed that it was better to sample and steal from the Tuscan poet than merely to imitate him.

Dante Goes
to the Movies

Dante is a vernacular writer for the Italians: one who sought to recreate the speech of the streets but also to tell tales in the oral tradition of Italy. Vernacular distinguished the work of the Italian poet and film director Pier Paolo Pasolini, who between 1963 and 1965 rewrote *The Divine Comedy* to form a critique of Italy's consumer society. Only the first two cantos of his prose poem were completed; Pasolini prepared these for publication in the form of a manuscript retrieved by chance from a desk drawer. ('I give these pages to the printers as a "document", but also to spite my "enemies": in fact, by offering them one more reason to despise me, I offer them one more reason to go to Hell.') *La divina mimesis* was published posthumously a week after Pasolini's murder in 1975, at the age of fifty-three.

The book bristles with the author's abhorrence of American-influenced materialism, religious cynicism and political opportunism. Like Dante before him ('O abject Italy, O seat of sorrow'), Pasolini fulminated against politicians and other dismal individuals who he believed had led his country to ruin. The cantos were conceived by Pasolini as part of a Dantesque journey through the 'Hell' of Italian neocapitalism. The first canto finds the author in a very dark moment of his life (*'un momento molto oscuro della mia vita'*). We are on the outskirts of Rome in a *borgata* or suburb-village just off the unlovely Viale Gregorio VII, an autostrada. It is a Sunday morning in April, perhaps Eastertide; the middle-aged Pasolini is lost like a 'castaway' (*naufrago*) and in despair until he meets his Virgilian guide. The guide turns out not to be Virgil but Pasolini himself, or rather a younger Pasolini from the 1950s, when he was hopeful of Italy's future and buoyed up by a Catholic-Gramscian political ideology. To the older Pasolini his younger self announces: '*Sono un' ombra*' ('I am a shade'), and in the dialogue that ensues we learn much about this Pasolini of ten years earlier. Like Dante, he had been a dialect poet, whose courtly, troubadour-inspired verse was written in the Latin-based

Friulian dialect spoken in parts of north-eastern Italy.

After graduating in literature from Bologna University in 1943, Pasolini moved with his parents to Casarsa della Delizia, a small town in Friuli near the Yugoslavian border. His *friulano* vernacular verse from this time, suffused with an elegiac sorrow, was political in intent. Fascism was hostile to Italy's dialectal variety (and, by extension, to Dante's own linguistic hybridity) as it threatened to undermine conformity and obedience to the glory that was Mussolini's Rome. Dialect poetry's very presence, however, would, in Gramscian terms, make the peasant farming communities of Friuli 'historically aware'; and he, Pasolini, would be the acknowledged legislator of their awareness. Pasolini's might have been a youthful presumption had he not discovered the work of Gramsci.

Close to Gramsci's heart was the question of a 'popular nationalist literature', which would incorporate marginalized Italian peoples and their dialects. A similar aspiration had stirred Dante to write *De vulgari eloquentia* six centuries earlier. On his arrival in Rome in the mid-1950s, Pasolini hoped to merge the lives and the language of the Friulian poor with those of the Roman poor. To that end he championed the disinherited and damned of post-war Rome, and allied Gramsci's intellectual leftism with a Dante-like Franciscan Catholicism. (Blessed are the poor, for they are exempt from the unholy Trinity of materialism, rationalism and property.) At heart, Pasolini's was a fierce pauperist Catholicism, in which the church was to be judged, not by its wealth, but by the standard of Christ and the Gospels. His best-known film, *The Gospel According to Matthew* (1964), was dedicated to John XXIII, the first pope to have opened up a dialogue between Catholicism and Marxism. (The word 'saint' was pointedly omitted from the title.)

The novel that made Pasolini famous, *Ragazzi di vita* ('The Street Kids'), published in 1955, recounts the spiral downwards into crime of a group of youths in post-war Rome. Much of the novel was written in *romanesco* dialect in order to remind Italy of a language that Pasolini believed it had largely ignored. It was part of his lifelong polemic against what he called '*la lingua dei padroni*', the language of the bosses. Here again Dante's influence is felt. For all that Dante wrote *The Divine Comedy* in Florentine dialect, Dante was interested in the myriad sub-languages from which that dialect evolved: jargons, specialized tongues, foreign idioms, Arabic, Provençal, Sicilian; above all Latin, Florentine's source-language. Dante's 'plurilingualism' (as the Italian linguist Gianfranco Contini famously termed it) profoundly influenced Pasolini's vernacular art with its hybrid registers of 'high' and 'low'. *La ricotta,* his thirty-five-minute episode in the collaborative film *RoGoPag* (1963), merges cha-cha songs and Charlie Chaplin routines with Bach and other Baroque music. Orson Welles plays an American director shooting a film about Christ's Passion on the bleak periphery of Rome. Over a tableau vivant inspired by Baroque paintings of the Deposition by Pontormo and Giovanni Battisti di Jacopo, Welles cries out like a Dante devil-fiend: 'Get those crucified bastards out of here!' The Roman who plays the part of the good thief, Stracci (Rags), dies while tied up on the cross under a broiling sun; he is one of Pasolini's many Caravaggio-like *figurae Christi* from this time. The director's second Roman film, the magnificent 1962 *Mamma Roma* starring Anna Magnani, ends as the hero lies dying in restraints on a prison bed like the dead Christ of Mantegna. The scene, suffused with a brooding darkness, is preceded by an episode where a dignified-looking Sardinian prison inmate (a nod perhaps to the Sardinian-born Gramsci?) recites from canto 4 of the *Inferno*; Dante is shaken out of sleep by a thunderclap before it dawns on him that he is in a prison-Limbo.

By the time Pasolini came to write *The Divine Mimesis,* his Dantesque dream of linguistic 'diversity' for post-war Italy was compromised. *Mamma Roma,* more so than any of Pasolini's early Roman vernacular works, caught the new mood in Italy as the 'economic miracle' of the mid-1960s brought chewing gum, Coca Cola and other trappings of consumerism to the *borgate.* But, like Dante's despised incomers to pre-Renaissance Florence (who, in Dante's estimation, set out to defraud and bilk others of their money), the Roman poor had become greedy for material gain and lost their pre-industrial innocence.

Pasolini's view – in some ways puritanically conservative – was shared by many Italian intellectuals in the mid-1960s, among them the film maker Michelangelo Antonioni. While Pasolini was at work on *The Divine Mimesis,* Antonioni was directing his bitingly political film *Red Desert* (1964), which opens with an image of industrial smokestacks and refineries billowing smoke somewhere in the consumer-capitalist north of Italy. A beautiful copper-haired woman (Monica Vitti, Antonioni's partner at the time) walks with a boy alongside a ditch while sounds of industrial grating and rhythmic machine-hissing thicken the infernal atmosphere. The industrial sumplands smouldering with yellow fumes are the price (Antonioni seems to be saying) to be paid for Italy's new-found affluence. The final scene unfolds on Ravenna's Via Alighieri, where Dante lies buried in a forbidding-looking domed tomb. (*'Dantis Poetae Sepulchrum'.)*

Pasolini believed that television was fast replacing Italy's multifarious dialects with a consumer Esperanto made up of garbled Americanisms and other linguistic imports. So much so, he wrote in 1974 on the eve of his murder, that if he wanted to remake one of his early Roman films he would be unable to do so as *romanesco* had all but disappeared. He gave the name 'aphasia' to the phenomenon: speechlessness.

The rent boy who murdered Pasolini had, it seems, been seduced by the *miracolo italiano* and its promise of a consumer idyll. Pino ('Joey the Toad') Pelosi was part of a generation of migrants newly arrived in Rome from the impoverished south, bringing with them their own dialects and moralities. The *borgata* where he lived, the Fascist-era Tiburtino III, retained something of the unspoiled semi-rural atmosphere of 'l'Italietta' (Italy's little homelands) so beloved of Pasolini. The outskirts, strewn with broken washbasins, chicken coops, prams, shoes and old tyres sprouting poppies, presented a Dantean pasticcio of the poetic and the squalid. Pelosi had sunk into crime for want of work and joined the MSI, Italy's main neo-Fascist party. Post-war Italy, in Pasolini's view, was 'a ship without a pilot in a great storm'

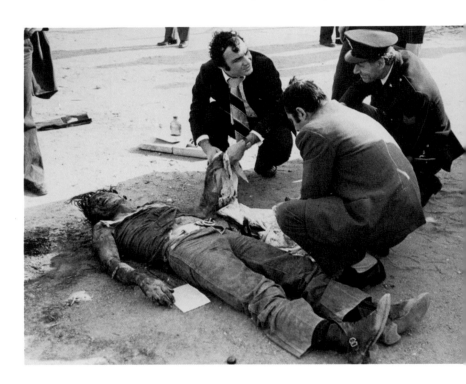

The scene of Pier Paolo Pasolini's murder on the sands of Idroscalo, Ostia, outside Rome, November 1975.

(*Purgatorio*, canto 6). In less than two decades Italy had ceased to be a peasant country and become one of the prime industrial nations of the West; the transformation, Pasolini genuinely believed, had rent society in a way that even Fascism had not.

The scene of Pasolini's murder, the shanty town of Idroscalo near Fiumicino airport, is a barren wasteland, where shacks lie scattered across a filthy blackened beach and in the distance rise the tenement slums of Nuova Ostia. Pelosi claimed that at least three other aggressors were present on the night of the murder. Who exactly they were remains a mystery even to Pelosi; however, they had 'strong Sicilian accents', he recalled many years later, and may have been known to Pasolini, who used the Sicilian city of Catania and the volcanic slopes of Mount Etna nearby as film locations. (Pasolini's 1968 movie *Teorema,* starring Terence Stamp, ends with a middle-aged man running naked across the black purgatorial sands of Etna, for all the world like Brunetto Latini's naked flight across those burning sands in canto 15 of the *Inferno*; Pasolini's later film *Porcile* is also partly set on Etna's black desert.) Reportedly, one of the aggressors had used the Catanian dialect word '*jarrusu*' (faggot) as he bludgeoned the director to death; Pasolini had been murdered to the accompaniment of a word from a dialect he had come to love.

Dante's influence on Pasolini was at its most profound in his 1957 verse epic, 'The Ashes of Gramsci'. Written in a Dantesque *terza rima*, the long poem revived the Italian tradition of nationalist 'civil poetry', which speaks in personal terms of the country's politics and history. Alone in the Protestant English cemetery in Rome adjacent to the Pyramid of Cestus (to which Shelley alludes in his 1821 elegy to Keats, 'Adonaïs'), Pasolini addresses his 'civil message' to the street walkers along the Tiber and the scrap-metal merchants of Testaccio. In the poem – one of the most audacious to emerge in Italy since the Second World War – Pasolini can only compare his emotional communion with

overleaf
1957: Pier Paolo Pasolini visiting Antonio Gramsci's tomb in the English Cemetery in Rome, where Keats and Shelley also lie buried.

the Roman poor to the youthful idealism of Shelley:

> …Ah how well
> I understand, silent in the wind's wet
> Humming, here where Rome is silent,
> Among wearily agitated cypresses,
> Next to you, Spirit whose inscription calls out
> Shelley…

The doleful cemetery music embodies a Catholic notion of death as a way to spiritual redemption. *Accattone* (1961), Pasolini's first film, opens with a quotation from *Purgatorio* canto 5: 'The angel of God took me…', and ends with the thief-hero Accattone ('beggar', in *romanesco*) murmuring as he lies moribund in a street after a road accident: '*Mo' sto bene*' – 'Now I'm all right'. From Rome's infernal thieving underworld Accattone has journeyed to a dimension of salvation and 'The merciful release I seek from death', as the poet Cavalcanti put it. The film, a work of astounding sensory realism, influenced Martin Scorsese and the young Bernardo Bertolucci.

Surprisingly, given its immense popularity, *The Divine Comedy* has rarely been filmed. In the early 1970s, the Florentine director Franco Zeffirelli asked Dustin Hoffman to star as Dante in a short film of the *Inferno*; the film was never made owing to lack of funds but the sketches and set designs are displayed now in the Zeffirelli Centre, which opened in Florence in 2017. Zeffirelli had seen the 1911 silent movie *L'Inferno*; directed by Francesco Bertolini, Giuseppe de Liguoro and Adolfo Padovan of Milano Films, the film took over three years to make and was perhaps the first true blockbuster; in the US alone it made $2 million – about $45 million in today's money, an extraordinary sum. The film's trio of Italian directors relied heavily for inspiration on the nineteenth-century French artist Gustave Doré's gloomy, neo-Gothic illustrations to Dante.

Poster for the 1911 Italian silent film *L'Inferno*. Virgil is dressed in white.

"Lasciate ogni speranza, voi ch'entrate"

LA DIVINA COMEDIA
"INFERNO,,
DELLA "MILANO FILMS,,
CONCESSIONARIO PER TVTTO IL MONDO
GVSTAVO LOMBARDO · NAPOLI

The film, a salmagundi of Gothic fantasia, mass writhing nudity and puffs of smoke (amid firecracker detonations), radiates a dark supra-reality. It contains scenes of such imagistic brilliance that one wonders why it has languished so long in cinematic purgatory as a precursor to the silent work of W. G. Griffith. For much of the time the camera remains static but into the frame leap leathery-winged devils brandishing tridents as the 'pious poet' Virgil attempts to fend them off. Beatrice, white-robed, hovers above-ground in a supernatural radiance. At one point Dante, recognizable from his medieval coif hat and flowing robe, contemplates the spectacle of the Prophet Muhammad as a bearded unfortunate trailing his entrails like onions on a string. While there is no explicit ban on figurative art in the Koran (representations of Muhammad appear in illuminated manuscripts up until the seventeenth century), *L'Inferno* is the only film on record to depict the Prophet thus eviscerated. In another stark scene, a crowd of poor naked bodies fights to board Charon's ferry in the hope of being taken to their particular place of torment. Like many of the damned in *L'Inferno,* they find a strange kind of fulfilment in embracing regions of sorrow, agony and pain. Charon clubs them back with an oar: they are too many. The Inca view of Hell as a freezing desert (where the damned have only stones to eat) might have looked something like this. The sinners' agonized physiognomies are hard to forget. Disappointingly, in 2004 the film was released on DVD with a soundtrack by the German electronic technicians Tangerine Dream; *kosmische* music, with its spacey sound clusters and pulseless drones, is soporific at the best of times: but the Dream score was melodramatic with bogus sung lyrics and a histrionic-sounding choir. At the film's end, Dante and Virgil are confronted by the comico-grotesque figure of Lucifer half-protruding from a sea of ice, his wings expanded and leathery. In his mouth he crunches the arch-traitors Brutus and Cassius (who betrayed

Caesar) and Judas Iscariot. Afterwards Dante and Virgil shimmy down Lucifer's ice-encrusted pelt from tuft to tuft before they creep through an opening in the rock and reach Purgatory. 'The Poets leave Hell. And again behold the stars', the caption explains. In less than a week, the audience is given to understand, Dante will carry his story back to the world above.

Dante's fusion of 'high' and 'low' speech intrigued the British film director Peter Greenaway who, eighty years after the release of *L'Inferno,* collaborated with the Clapham-born artist and Dante translator Tom Phillips on a video dramatization of the first eight cantos of the *Inferno*. Broadcast in the UK on Channel 4 in 1990, *A TV Dante* deployed state-of-the-art electronic media to recreate Dante's underworld. The 'dark wood' of the opening canto is a modern city at night, perhaps the urban jungle of New York, with police car sirens just audible. A computerized leopard slouches across the screen, followed by a lion and a she-wolf; David Attenborough, the first of the film's many academic commentators, pops up to explain the reputation of wolves in medieval Europe. The mini-series gains much from the presence of John Gielgud as Virgil, who intones in grandiloquently sepulchral tones: 'This is the city of Despair...You that enter here, abandon hope', followed by a sound of despairing cries.

How to reconfigure Dante's poem for a short film? Stan Brakhage's mesmeric *The Dante Quartet*, completed in 1987, flickers like a Jackson Pollock painting come to life. The product of six years' work, the seven-minute film is a cinematic approximation of abstract expressionism, with swabs of blue, ruddy golds, reds and splashes of green pulsing and shifting on screen like a liquid stained glass window. Brakhage, one of America's most revered experimental film makers, said he wished to 'recreate' Dante's mind in a state of turmoil; the vividly-coloured paint, applied directly onto the film stock, creates such an effect of swirling thoughts that Dante emerges as a modern poet of interiority. The grim mausoleum night of the *Inferno* appears to have evaporated. 'Hell must be beautiful', Brakhage explained, 'otherwise people would not spend so much time there.'

Dante provided a different kind of vernacular in the work of the post-war American artist Robert Rauschenberg, a contemporary of Brakhage. Ingeniously, Rauschenberg superimposed images of golfers and weightlifters from back issues of *Sports Illustrated*, a *Life* magazine deodorant advert, *New York Herald Tribune* news media shots of John F. Kennedy and Richard Nixon onto smudgy watercolour, pencil and crayon backgrounds to conjure a twentieth-century Hades. His 'Thirty-Four Illustrations from Dante's Inferno' (1958–60), housed since 1963 at New York's MoMA, unforgettably enrich and reinterpret the *Inferno* in a contemporary American idiom. Rauschenberg used his famous 'solvent transfer method' to haunting effect: ghostly replicas of magazine illustrations were made by damping them with lighter fluid and rubbing them on the reverse side with a ballpoint. Charon's barge becomes a spectral oil freighter; the bituminous city of Dis, a conflagration of oil derricks and smoke stacks; and Virgil is a space-suited NASA test pilot.

For inspiration, Rauschenberg used John Ciardi's verse translation, *The Inferno*, which sold over half a million copies in its first six months of publication in the mid-1950s. Ciardi's was a sparse and stripped-down Dante, in which some American critics were pleased to detect a 'virile, tense American' vernacular. Though Rauschenberg spoke no Italian (and was moreover acutely dyslexic), he viewed Ciardi as his own 'Virgilian guide' through the late medieval poetry of the *Inferno*. In canto 21, Satan's sidekick Barbariccia breaks wind uproariously in Dante's presence; Rauschenberg used a 1959 *Life* photograph of gas-masked riot police in Nyasaland (now Malawi) to stand in for Barbariccia and his army of mischief-makers, among them Malacoda (Captain Stinkytail). It is possible to detect in the illustrations evidence of

Solvent transfer drawing of canto 4 of the *Inferno* by the postwar American artist Robert Rauschenberg. In the top right-hand corner, dimly visible, is a photograph of Constantine's Arch in Rome, taken from a 1958 *Sports Illustrated*.

racialism and an awkward homosexuality. In some of the thirty-four pictures, pointedly, Africans and East Asians susceptible to Soviet influence are made to represent Dante's most demonic and wildly obscene hell-pit tormentors. Rauschenberg, a gay man at work in a homophobic America, was troubled by Dante's portrayal of his teacher and mentor Brunetto Latini as a sexual deviant adrift in Hell. Without any forensic evidence of his own, Dante besmirches Latini's reputation for all time. (To this day, thanks to Dante, Latini is remembered more as a sodomite than as a great thirteenth-century humanist and civic hero of Florence.) The penalty for Latini's presumed homosexuality 'might not have bothered Dante', said Rauschenberg, 'but it bothered me'. In the solvent transfer picture, Latini is represented by the champion hurdler and sprinter Glenn Davis, photographed in mid-leap by a *Time* reporter. Maybe Rauschenberg wished to make a covert link between Olympic athletes and the homosexual community –

a shared emphasis on the body beautiful and bath-house culture of 1950s America. Or perhaps Latini is merely the 'winner' of that particular hurdle race.

One might ask what a Texas-born, Neo-Dada maverick and likely atheist saw in Dante. Rauschenberg had no interest in Dante scholarship, and confessed an 'impatience' with the poet's Christian 'moralizing'. (His parents were Fundamentalist Christians.) The abysmal atmosphere of Dante's Hell, with its spectral wanderers and iced-over regions of the afterlife, may well have resonated with a United States riven by race riots and Cold War antagonisms. In 1956, two years after the appearance of Ciardi's translation, the Soviet leader Nikita Khrushchev denounced Stalin and his 'cult of personality'. The Stalinist 'purge trials' of the 1930s (as finally acknowledged by Khrushchev) find expression in the Rauschenberg cycle, where an image of the Soviet Ministry for Foreign Affairs stands in for the Gates of Hell of canto 3. The Soviet Union under Khrushchev seemed to embody the scientific astonishment and discovery of the late 1950s, when the first Sputnik was lobbed into space and a new age dawned of sleek Zil cars, gadgets and 'gracious living'. A flavour of this scientific adventurism informs Rauschenberg's Dante cycle. The work was a signpost in his development as a post-abstract expressionist; it prepared the way for his triumph at the Venice Biennale in the summer of 1964, when he won the Grand Prize, and established him as rather more than a Pop purveyor of stuffed animals, painted beds and objects found on the New York sidewalks.

Exaggeratedly God-fearing, Gustave Doré's illustrations to *The Divine Comedy* remain unequalled for their portrayal of Gothic horror and celestial glories alike. Rauschenberg said he 'hated' them: there was too much crude thunder-psalm and brute ugliness in them for his liking. Doré's *Divine Comedy*, first published in 1868 by the French publishers Hachette, was

Gustave Doré's Dante-like visualisation of the Seven Dials slum in Covent Garden, London. From Blanchard Jerrold's 1872 book of social reportage, *London: A Pilgrimage.*

a gigantic, grim-looking tome with gold-leaf page edges. An instant bestseller, it made Doré the most successful and famous illustrator of his day. Yet it was not Doré's finest moment. A year later, in 1869, the English journalist Blanchard Jerrold invited Doré to collaborate with him on a book about London. Appearing in 1872, *London: A Pilgrimage* unfolds as a Dantean journey or 'pilgrimage' through a place of religious awe and terror. Doré's engravings reveal a shadow world of bone-grubbers, flower-hawkers, ice-vendors, gin-drinkers and other waifs of the perceived lowest end of human life. Jerrold accompanies Doré-Virgil through a metropolitan underworld where prostitutes speak of swift and joyless financial transactions conducted in the rookeries off Fleet Street. Images of poverty and social damnation flicker like a magic lantern show. Over Jerrold's vision of London as an over-crowded labour market hovers the spirit of Dante, whose influence on Victorian literature was immense. James Thomson's long, fretful jeremiad of a poem, *The City of Dreadful Night,* written between 1870 and 1874, is rife with imagery from the *Inferno.* Through the death-still streets of the benighted city of the title (it could be London, it could be Glasgow) the Scottish-born Thomson wanders haggard with insomnia. Thomson was, as W. B. Yeats said of Dante, a 'Daimonic Man', driven by a daemon to write (as well as drink). The poem takes its epigraph from canto 3 of the *Inferno*: *Per me si va nella città dolente* ('Through me is the way into the city of pain'). In the course of his urban wanderings Thomson encounters an angry old man dragging himself like a Beckett character through a ditch in search of childhood's long-gone innocence. The poem's shadowlike imagery of 'savage woods' and 'baleful glooms' left its mark on T. S. Eliot when he came to write *The Waste Land,* a poem brocaded with Thomsonian images of drought and sterility.

The long shadow cast by Dante on Western literature – unbroken since the fourteenth century – reaches a moment of luminous intensity in Malcolm Lowry's masterpiece *Under the Volcano* (1947). Set in Cuernavaca on the Day of the Dead, the novel describes the last twenty-four hours in the life of Geoffrey Firmin, His Majesty's ex-consul, as he drowns in liquor and despair under the shadow of the Popocatapetl volcano. Lowry's genius was to transform Firmin's addiction into a parable of universal significance. In prose of a Joycean ripeness Lowry explores the uncertain human condition of us all. Through the lens of his own alcohol addiction Lowry asks what it is to be human, and how we might overcome human weakness. These are properly Dantean themes. Often in the *Inferno* sinners are described as 'following appetites like beasts' (*seguendo come bestie l'appetito*). Old cravings are re-quickened in them as they crawl through shadows and sheets of rain, poor fools stewing in the mess of their own sins.

Lowry's alcoholic ex-consul is himself unable to 'make purgation' because he is half in love with damnation: his own. Lowry intended that all his writing – three unfinished novels, six or seven short stories, hundreds of letters and poems – should be part of a great continuum called *The Voyage that Never Ends*, with the Mexican masterwork at its centre. Only fragments of this scheme remain, but Lowry's hallucinatory 1935 novella *Lunar Caustic*, based on his treatment for addiction in Bellevue mental hospital, New York, was to represent Purgatory. In some way, Firmin's Mexican Hell mirrored Lowry's Hell, for Lowry wrote in the tradition of the doomed poet who sees an exaltation in damnation: James Thomson, Hart Crane, Edgar Allen Poe, Arthur Rimbaud and others in 'Alcoholics Hieronymous Bosch', as Lowry punned of that sulphurous crew. He died in 1957 at the age of 48, from an overdose of barbiturates, having lurched from one worse relapse and heavier fall to another.

Among the greatest interpreters of Dante in modern times are the Irish. Dante is mentioned ninety times in W. B. Yeats's published prose, adapted in ten of his poems and three of his plays. Yeats's one sustained effort at Dantesque composition, 'Cuchulain Comforted', considers the Irish mythological hero as he strides 'among the dead' in the afterlife – a world of languorous flame and woeful shades that gives an impression of something flitting and unfixed. The poem was written in Dantescan *terza rima* two weeks before Yeats died in 1939. Five years earlier, in 1934, his compatriot Samuel Beckett published his debut story collection *More Pricks than Kicks*. The opening story, 'Dante and the Lobster', introduced the hard-drinking, Gorgonzola-eating Dublin student Belacqua Shuah, named after the Florentine lute-maker Belacqua of *Purgatorio* canto 4. Dante finds Belacqua slumped under a large rock with other souls condemned to wait for as long as they have waited in life to repent their ways. The process of their purgation may take hundreds of years, with long periods of waiting on different terraces of Mount Purgatory. Belacqua, inured to sloth, provided Beckett with a literary model for 'waiting' as a condition of human existence. "For some strange reason I was certainly fascinated very early by the character and went to a lot of trouble to find out about him", Beckett wrote of Belacqua in letter of 1958, adding: "But little seems to be known, except that he was a lute-maker in Florence, a friend of Dante and notorious for his indolence and apathy.' In Beckett's punctuation-free novel *How It Is* (published in 1961) Belacqua is very much the Beckettian *homo patiens,* sinking progressively into immobility: 'Belacqua fallen over on his side tired of waiting...' Beckett wrote. The greatness of Beckett's writing can no more be divorced from a religious awareness of death and dying than can Dante's. How do we judge human behaviour? What is important in a life – or a death? The hermetic sparsities of Beckett's prose communicate a sense of God's absence and of lives long since blanked out and done. His 1933 poem 'Malacoda' evokes the unutterable sadness of his father's death. The bowler-hatted undertakers who come to coffin and remove the body are likened to the 'clawed demons' or *malebranche* of the *Inferno* (one of which, 'Malacoda', provides the poem with its title).

If Gustave Doré makes us feel the inky darkness of Hell, Sandro Botticelli adopted a calm graphic style for his Dante illustrations, which have their own kind of humour. Rauschenberg admired them greatly, as did Beckett (who was annoyed to have missed the 1965 exhibition in Berlin of Rauschenberg's Dante cycle). Commissioned by the Medici banking family in 1480, Botticelli's beautiful, dreamily surreal visualizations of *The Divine Comedy* were executed in brown ink on vellum calf skin. The depiction of Belacqua with his arms clasped tight round his knees in the foetal posture fascinated Beckett. The drawn lines, fine as spider's silk, are a marvel of precise Renaissance *disegno*. Beckett's early short story, 'Echo's Bones' (intended as the 'fagpiece' or final story for *More Pricks than Kicks)* again featured Belacqua who, having died in hospital under surgery, is returned to life in a Dantean netherworld haunted by freakish shades, among them a fairytale giant called Lord Gall of Wormwood who wears a tasselled red fez.

Rauschenberg observed that there was an element of the 'cartoon' in Botticelli's Dante illustrations. As in a graphic novel or stop-start animation, the pilgrim-poet often appears several times in the same image. By resisting the lurid imagery Dante seems to call for, Botticelli arrived at 'pictorial propriety' (as Walter Pater called it). The zoological exactitude of the membranes, bones, joints and claws of Botticelli's Lucifer and his giant bat wings recall the anatomical sketches of the artist's contemporary Leonardo da Vinci. A plan to colour in all the drawings surely did exist; but only four of the ninety-two large vellum pages (that we know of) were pigmented. Many of Botticelli's illustrations seem peculiarly modern; freed at last from bodily existence, Dante floats zenithwards with Beatrice through the biblical River of

overleaf
From Sandro Botticelli's illustrations to *The Divine Comedy*. Dante and Virgil are each shown six times as they descend through the eighth circle of Hell, as in a modern stop-start animation.

Light, from galaxy to galaxy and silver star to silver star. Dante's *alta fantasia* ('high fantasy') is here positively psychedelic. As Beatrice turns her lovely head to the poet, his arms are raised, and his face is a mask of drugged consternation.

Dante inspired many late eighteenth-century British artists – from William Blake to Henry Fuseli. But the most graceful and sinuous of Dante illustrations were those by the York-born neoclassical draughtsman and sculptor John Flaxman. Pared down and restrained to the point of severity, these convey a maximum of drama with the minimum of means. In 1787 the diminutive, hunchbacked artist left for the Continent; during his seven years in Rome he became a master of the concise outline which he had perfected earlier while working for Josiah Wedgwood the potter. Flaxman's Dante illustrations, appearing first in Rome in 1802, exerted a huge influence on Continental artists such as David and Goya. They were published in London in 1807 in a book, *Compositions by John Flaxman, Sculptor, R.A., from the Divine Poem of Dante Alighieri, containing Hell, Purgatory and Paradise.* The book speaks to experiences – loss, uncertainty, dread, sorrow, bereavement, love – that all humans must have. Beatrice moves across the pages like a phantom, the flowing lines of her robes suggesting the decorative reliefs on classical Greek vases and freezes: simple, neo-Attic lines, no shadow. Lucifer is a gargoyle-like monster in heavenly accentuated outline, while Belacqua, curled up like a child, sits in an agony of waiting. Just as Dante's search for self-knowledge had ended in Heaven, so Flaxman's mysteriously abstract 'The Beatific Vision' concludes his reading of *Paradiso.* Here the radiant circles of Paradise are etched in the faintest of black marks like tiny piano keys. Outlined in dots at the very centre is God. The strangeness of the design anticipates science fiction.

Inevitably, popular reworkings of Dante have concentrated on 'the man who travelled to Hell'. For the Gothic Revivalists

*Un punto vidi che raggiava lume
Acuto sì, che 'l viso ch' egli affoca,
Chiuder conviensi per lo forte acume.
Paradiso Canto
28.*

John Flaxman's vision of Dante's canto 28, *Paradiso*. The pilgrim views God as an infinitely bright point at the centre of the universe.

overleaf
The Thieves' Punishment by Henry Fuseli, 1772, inspired by canto 25 of the *Inferno*, where Dante and Virgil encounter thieves being attacked by snakes.

Dante held all manner of lurid fascinations. Henry Fuseli, Flaxman's contemporary 'sublime' master, executed five paintings and thirteen drawings based on the *Inferno*. Fuseli was attracted to German 'Sturm und Drang' notions of inchoate terror. (He was born a German speaker in Zurich in 1741.) 'The Thieves' Punishment', completed in 1772, shows the thieves of cantos 24–5 metamorphosed into low creeping serpents. Bent as he was on death and the necromantic imagination, there is only one drawing by Fuseli on a subject from *Purgatorio* (and none at all from *Paradiso*). Fuseli's friend William Blake was another who divined a dark supernatural element in Dante.

Blake was pretty well forgotten when he died in London in 1827; a single mysterious poem, 'The Tyger', had reached the anthologies, but his reputation as an artist was at a low ebb. Unfinished at the time of his death, Blake's *Divine Comedy* illustrations were seen at the time as the work of a 'madman'. Through excruciating gall-bladder attacks Blake the artist-poet sat bent over his drawing book, and managed to produce 102 watercolours, some of them not much more than pencil indications. Taken together, they add emphasis to Dante's moral condemnation of materialism and money-making, which appealed to the Blake who had spoken out against the dark satanic mills of proto-capitalist England. Unquestionably Blake saw himself as Dante's equal. Scenes of watery flame and rapture coexist in the illustrations with scenes of scorching flame and a savage wilderness of pain. Blake's flaming imagination, like Fuseli's, was better suited to conveying infernal panoramas. Yet his *Paradiso* ranks as the greatest response to Dante's Elysium by any British artist; for Yeats they were simply the 'crowning work' of Blake's life. Paradise, Dante tells us, is beyond night and day; it is light itself, an idea conveyed by Blake in his beautiful 'Beatrice on the Car, Matilda and Dante', which is suffused with a rainbow radiance and spirit of mystical pantheism. Across great fields of light Beatrice stands imperious in the chariot pulled by a gryphon.

After Beckett and Lowry, *The Divine Comedy* became a touchstone for high modernist experiment in the work of William Burroughs. The avant-garde American author and reformed heroin junkie had first read Dante in John Ciardi's translation of 1954. His best-known novel *Naked Lunch* (1959) contains passages of Dante-like scatology and outbursts of rhetorically elegant fury. By bringing the surreal drama of the *Inferno* to bear on contemporary America, Burroughs set out to shock. His dizzying 1960s trilogy of cut-up novels – *The Soft Machine, The Ticket That Exploded, Nova Express* – jettisoned conventional narrative for arbitrarily juxtaposed 'cut-ups' from newspapers, pulp sci-fi fanzines, travelogue and pages of hauntingly beautiful prose-poetry. The collision of 'high' and 'low' culture was Dantean in its way. Appropriately, the first witness for the defence at the *Naked Lunch* obscenity trial (which took place in Massachusetts in 1965) was Ciardi; a poet as well as a translator who had taught Frank O'Hara creative writing at Harvard, Ciardi argued that themes of sex and excretion in Burroughs were as necessary to his dystopian vision as they were to Dante's. Count Ugolino's cannibalism in the *Inferno* was not so dissimilar, Ciardi argued, to the scene in *Naked Lunch* where a Southern sheriff makes a savage meal of an African American prisoner ('Nothing like a good *slow* Nigga Burnin"). The Massachusetts Supreme Court's ruling on 7 July 1966 that *Naked Lunch* was not, after all, obscene effectively marked the end of literary censorship in the United States. It may be that what shocks one generation is accepted quite calmly by the next.

Burroughs had, as it says in the song, let the dogs out, but Dante's reimaging was if anything more radical in the hands of the African–American playwright and poet LeRoi Jones (who, in 1965, changed his name to Amiri Baraka in solidarity with the assassinated black rights activist Malcolm X). Jones's 1965 novel *The System of Dante's Hell* took its title from John D. Sinclair's 1939 prose translation of the *Inferno*. Under the heading 'The System of Dante's Hell', Sinclair had explained how the poet's Hell is divided into strata upon substrata of sinners. Based on Sinclair's exposition Jones created a Burroughs-like impasto of cut-ups and disjointed grammar. He was writing chiefly about the Hell of growing up as a black man in segregated America. Hell is where white people refuse to see him as anything other than a 'Negro'. Dantesque echoes abound. 'On a porch that summer, in night, in my body's skin, drunk, sitting stiff-legged in a rocking chair. Vita nuova.' The reference to Dante's youthful memoir underscores the fact that the black teenager LeRoi has entered a difficult 'new life': he has come of age as a homosexual (though LeRoi had a gay episode early on with the poet Frank O'Hara, in later life he became defiantly macho and even rather homophobic). The staccato prose was intended to reflect the disunity of an American 'Hell run by devils' or a white 'Devil America'. The novel had no sooner appeared than race riots broke out in 1965 in the Watts ghetto of Los Angeles. That year of 1965 happened to be an important year for Dante studies. *Life* magazine invited Rauschenberg to commemorate the 700th anniversary of Dante's birth in 1265 with a six-page pullout panorama of the artist's vision of Hell on earth. It included a photograph of a Ku Klux Klansman in robes and hood displaying a hangman's noose from his car window. Dante, always our contemporary, spoke to the frightening uncertainties of 1960s America.

In the centuries since the 1300s we have lost Dante's sense of Heaven and Hell. Yet Dante's ghost is present in so much modern self-portraiture in lyric poetry, fiction, film, art and memoir. The Argentine fabulist Jorge Luis Borges learned a good deal from Dante about economy, directness and visual precision. His most characteristic story, 'The Library of Babel', is a dry run for his ambition (never realized) to write a novel about the universe that would contain the multiplicity of all books. On his death in 1986 Borges left behind 100-odd slender fictions and as many poems – but no novels. Compared with the blockbusting authors of our age, this was a small (if perfectly formed) output. By his own account, Borges first read *The Divine Comedy* in the early 1940s in Dent's bilingual Italian-English edition. He read it on the tram that took him every day to his job as municipal assistant librarian in Buenos Aires during the Perón dictatorship. 'I began Hell in English', he recollected. 'By the time I reached Paradise I could follow Dante in Italian.' Having thus mastered Dante, Borges hazarded the provocation that the entire *Divine Comedy* had been undertaken to allow Dante to stage an imagined encounter with the dead woman who had rejected him: Beatrice. Acutely myopic as a child, Borges at about this time went blind; inhabiting his own dark inner world, 'Georgie' created the gems of laconic wit and invention contained in the volumes *Ficciones* and *El Aleph*, published in 1944 and 1949 respectively. Argentina was in political turmoil. Borges openly scorned Perónism and the Spanish-American tradition of the *caudillo* (strongman leader) manifest in the crowd-pleasing populism of Perón and his wife Evita. For his troubles, in 1946 Borges was demoted from librarian to municipal poultry inspector. He continued to study Dante at the Palacio Barolo library, designed by the Italian architect Mario Palanti as a tribute to *The Divine Comedy* (complete with lifts representing each of the poem's seven deadly sins). Borges' final months were spent in Geneva in a residence with no name or number on the door; there was little to disturb the writer's peace save the bells from nearby St Pierre cathedral. *Dan-te, Dan-te, Dan-te,* they chimed.

Life after
Dante's Death

Dante Alighieri has been dead for 700 years. The date of his death, 14 September 1321, is one of the few surviving facts about him. He expired of a fever while on a diplomatic mission to Venice, scholars believe, and was buried with honour at the church of San Pier Maggiore in Ravenna. Dante died as he was born, a Catholic in faith, though his life had scarcely been a blameless one that eschewed vice. In *Purgatorio* Beatrice had berated him for his perceived moral failings. Prone to bouts of self-delusion, prideful and overweening, Dante was a conflictedly human soul.

Within a year of his death at the age of fifty-six, commentaries on *The Divine Comedy* had begun to appear. The earliest extant commentary, by Dante's son Jacopo Alighieri, can be dated to 1322. A work of filial devotion, it seeks to clarify in rudimentary terms the 'illustrious' poet's 'profound and real intentions', but not much more. Soon after, commentaries appeared in Italian cities as far apart as Genoa, Naples, Pisa and Verona, a testament to the poem's national prominence. Dante's second son, Pietro Alighieri, offered a more learned gloss fifteen years after Jacopo's. It insisted on *The Divine Comedy*'s status as a poetic fiction or *fictio*; Dante, by this estimation, was the sort of writer who might have enjoyed the etymology of the word 'fiction' from the Latin *fingere,* to 'mould' or 'contrive'. In the Middle Ages there was no more significant recognition of an author's *auctoritas* – authority – than for his writings to be thus explicated. A little later in the fourteenth century Giovanni Boccaccio, who was forty-eight years younger than Dante, inaugurated the practice (still widespread in Italy) of giving public *lecturae Dantis* or Dante lectures.

Between October 1373 and January 1374 Boccaccio gave a total of sixty lectures on '*il Dante*' (as *The Divine Comedy* was then known). The poem was by now the most popular book in Italy after the Bible: commissioned by the Florentine Republic, the lectures drew in the Latin-educated elite as well as the vernacular-literate. Unfortunately for Florence, Boccaccio fell mortally ill and abandoned his lectures at canto 17 of the *Inferno*. (He died in 1375, a year after Petrarch.) The notes he made on those cantos became known as the *Esposizioni sopra la Commedia* (Expositions on the Comedy). They championed Dante's *fiorentinità* (Florentine-ness) and mighty vindication of the 'vulgar'.

Typically as *lector Dantis* Boccaccio delighted in using rough tavern talk. His lexical assault on the gluttonous in canto 6 of the *Inferno* recalls his earlier description of the dissolute Friar Cipolla in the *Decameron*, a shabby character even by Boccaccio's standards, who gulls his adoring congregation into believing that he has the power to show them a feather from the wings of the archangel Gabriel (the story became the basis for Thomas Mann's novella *Mario and the Magician*):

> All these, then, are guzzlers, gorgers, gulpers, yearners, grabbers, slobberers, bitches, twitters, howlers, belchers; they are intemperate, oily, dirty, filthy, foul, wheezing, dribbling and nauseating men who are disgusting and harmful to see and hear. No: they are not men, but rather beasts.

The vernacular literature of Europe would have to wait until François Rabelais in the sixteenth century for such exuberant verbal invention.

During his three months as lecturer, Boccaccio extolled a '*poeta-theologus*', whose spiritual journey through the afterlife was a divinely authorized attempt to explain the meaning and purpose of life. Many others saw a superhuman authorship in *The Divine Comedy* (Heaven had set its hand upon the poem). In a famous letter to his patron in Verona, Cangrande della Scala, Dante explained that the poem's true purpose was to 'remove those living in this life from a state of misery and bring them to a state of felicity'. (Though the letter cannot be attributed to Dante on genuine authority it does sound Dantescan.) Boccaccio's

overleaf Six Tuscan Poets *by Giorgio Vasari, 1544. From right to left: Cavalcanti, Dante, Boccaccio and (in white and red) Petrarch. Behind Petrarch are the humanist scholars Cristoforo Landino and Marsilio Ficino. The last two figures have also been identified as Cino da Pistoia and Guittone d'Arezzo.*

biography of Dante, written in the early 1350s, portrayed a conscientious man of 'moderate appetites' but of occasionally dark-hearted passions. It is to Boccaccio, incidentally, that we owe the identification of Beatrice with 'Bice' Portinari, a young girl 'full gentle and winning in her ways'.

The *Decameron*, Boccaccio's masterwork, was completed in Florence in around 1352 two decades before the Dante lectures. The book's 100 *novelle* – loosely, 'fables' or 'histories' – tell of card sharps, lubricious clergymen, wicked tax collectors, cheating merchant bankers and other shady types who elude punishment even as they dupe their next victim. 'Getting away with it' – a much-valued skill among bankers in medieval Italy – is one of the great unstated themes of the *Decameron*. Boccaccio's confidence-trickster priests, the very embodiment of *furbizia* or clever rascality, are seen to indulge the flagrantly un-Christian practice of lying from the pulpit as they hoodwink their way to power and sexual gratification. They would surely have ended up among the stink-snakes of the *Inferno*.

The stories are narrated over a period of ten days (hence the title *Decameron*) by a company of 'nobly born' young men and women who have escaped plague-stricken Florence in 1348. In the hills above the city, in Fiesole, they chance on a paradisal garden where, in between telling stories, they flirt, laugh and take turns to serenade each other on the lute. The Arcadian setting, influenced by Dante's vision of the Garden of Eden in *Purgatorio*, contrasts with the hellish descriptions of pestilence back in the Tuscan capital where, we are told, 'things had come to such a pass that dead human beings were treated no better than goats.' Though Dante is not a character in the *Decameron*, his presence is felt throughout. Along with his fellow Tuscan poets Guido Cavalcanti and Cino da Pistoia, Dante is mentioned in the introduction to the Fourth Day of stories, while the tale about the spendthrift Nastagio degli Onesti (Fifth Day) effectively recasts the episode of the squanderers in canto 13 of the *Inferno*. There are many characters, beginning with Pope Boniface VIII, who are common to both the *The Divine Comedy* and the *Decameron*. Moreover, Boccaccio's book is a human comedy (the first word of the *Decameron* is '*Umana*', Human) in the way that *The Divine Comedy* is a human comedy: foul and horrible at the start, but in the end felicitous, as the noble men and women acquire a better understanding of the world through their storytelling.

In some way, Boccaccio's book is a moral education. Time and again, the ten-strong band of storytellers insist on the educational potential of their tales, their function as moral exempla. 'Good stories are always instructive', Elissa proclaims, 'and should be listened to attentively, whoever is telling them.' If fiction is unable to exert an influence on the affairs of the world directly, perhaps – like a folk tale – it can serve as a teaching device. Dante, in trusting that *The Divine Comedy* would bring readers to a 'state of felicity', thought much the same. Beneath the *Decameron*'s mixture of the coarse, funny and fabulous was an author who had witnessed the Black Death in his native Tuscany and lost his own father, a prosperous Florentine merchant-banker, to the '*mortifera pestilenza*'.

Boccaccio's rowdy pomp conceals a very Dantean element of pilgrimage. The nobles leave Florence by way of Santa Maria Novella church (completed in 1360, forty years after Dante's death), and set aside two Fridays during their storytelling to remember Christ's death as well as two Saturdays to remember the Blessed Virgin. The funniest of the *novelle* turn on a practical joke or *beffa* of some sort. Two money-lenders wonder how best to dispose of a dead body concealed in a trunk. The macabre whimsy looks forward to Renaissance comedy and, beyond that, to farce such as the 'Kipper and the Corpse' episode of *Fawlty Towers*. Boccaccio's openness about sex, a possible antidote to the furtive worm of pornography, was ahead of its time. In his 1971 film *Il Decamerone*

Pier Paolo Pasolini captured something of the book's exuberance, only to be branded a 'pornographer' by some critics.

Among the *Decameron*'s many dubious characters are moneygrubbers who think nothing of fleecing the public. Landolfo Rufolo, after squandering his money on the stock market, decides to become a pirate, and 'devote himself to making other people's property his own'. Boccaccio had been apprenticed to the Compagnia dei Bardi banking house of Florence, the Lehman Brothers of its day, which virtually collapsed after clients (among them King Edward III of England) defaulted on their loans. Boccaccio was left with a lifelong distate for money-making and 'wild spending' in general. The pestilential Florence of Boccaccio's birth had been no less corrupted by the florin than had Dante's.

As the 1450s gave way to the 1460s, so Dante's political pre-eminence in Florence was strengthened by Lorenzo de' Medici. Scarcely twenty when he was appointed head of the Florentine Medici clan in 1469, Lorenzo 'the Magnificent' wrote Tuscan dialect sonnets in praise of falconry and an unfinished *terza rima* composition, the *Simposio*, which is almost parodically Dantean. The Florentine language was still in its infancy but Lorenzo devoutly hoped that one day it would grow and conquer hand in hand with the *fiorentio imperio* (Florentine empire). Under his rule, Dante was therefore co-opted into fulfilling a Ciceronian role of *optimus civis*, 'best citizen'; he was made a republican civic poet, selflessly active in the affairs of the Florentine Republic.

A milestone in the Florentine cult of Dante and the book market in Renaissance Europe for printed versions of his work was Cristofero Landino's 1481 edition of *The Divine Comedy*, complete with copper engravings based on Botticelli's Dante cycle and a lengthy commentary in the vernacular. For Landino, Dante's poem embodied all that was greatest about Florentine culture and potent tongue. Born in 1424, Landino was a high-minded humanist scholar and poet who wrote in exalted terms about Dante as a profoundly moral guide to life, one who 'thunders and rails against injustice, perfidy, incontinence, cruelty...and all other things.' He called for the outlawed and estranged Dante to be 'returned to his homeland after a long exile'. Florentines were aware that Dante had died and been buried in Ravenna, and that his dust was deserving of a proper memorial. In 1396 the Commonwealth of Florence petitioned Ravenna for the relocation of the poet's remains. The request was declined, as were others made in 1430 and 1476. In 1519 Pope Leo X considered yet another petition, by the Medicean Academy, endorsed by family descendants of Beatrice Portinari and by Michelangelo, who agreed to design and build a monument. The request was granted; but when the tomb was opened by Florentine emissaries all they found were dusty laurel leaves and bone fragments. The monumental nineteenth-century tomb built for Dante in the Basilica of Santa Croce in Florence remains empty to this day. It was unveiled in 1865 on the sixth centenary of the poet's birth.

It was not by chance that Landino's Dante appeared in Florence so soon after the April 1478 'Pazzi conspiracy' that dared to challenge Medicean supremacy. Amid a fury of dagger thrusts, Lorenzo de' Medici narrowly escaped assassination in the cathedral. For years the Pazzi banking clan had resented the Medicis' climb to power. The signal for the attack came just as the officiating priest raised the Host: Pazzi hirelings rushed in with knives drawn. Lorenzo managed to barricade himself behind the bronze sacristy doors and raise the alarm but his younger brother Giuliano died. Afterwards panic descended on the Tuscan capital as Medici enforcers cracked down on the presumed ringleaders. On Lorenzo's command, Pazzi family members were to be torn alive from groin to neck, and their widows banished to convents. In Mafia parlance this was a *regolamento di conti*, or 'balancing of accounts'. From his grandfather Cosimo de' Medici, the

merchant-poet Lorenzo had learned the art of how to wield and consolidate power.

The attack at High Mass only buttressed Medicean power and Lorenzo's reputation as a strongman. In the climate of heightened civic pride in Florence, inevitably Dante's name was tied ever more closely to Florentine supremacy and cultural attainment on the peninsula. The Landino edition was intended to reconfirm Lorenzo's power and serve as a riposte to the 'impudent' appropriation of Dante by non-Tuscans, among them the slyly watchful Pope Sixtus IV, who had favoured the Pazzi over the Medici as bankers to the Holy See, and probably backed the April plotters. Lorenzo had good reason to fear this pope. Having ruled despotically for two decades Lorenzo died prematurely in April 1492 (six months before Columbus 'discovered' America) at the age of forty-three, his physician having prescribed a concoction of pulverized pearls for gout. Afterwards the Medici dynasty petered out in the poltroon-like figure of Cosimo III, who presided over the Duchy of Tuscany for half a century until 1720. Under this sanctimonious man, all nude Renaissance statues were removed from the streets and Michelangelo's (unabashedly homoerotic) 'David' was concealed beneath a tarpaulin.

Lorenzo de' Medici was still in his thirties when, in 1482, Girolamo Savonarola arrived in Florence with plans to purge the city of financial malpractice and sexual sin. Understandably the Dominican friar has been compared to Dante, 'the first religious reformer', according to the poet Shelley. In Savonarola's view, Florence was a sham republic ruled by a banker-tyrant with monarchical pretensions (Lorenzo secretly referred to himself as Lorenzo Rex Medici). Savonarola called for a return to a New Testament ethics of religious poverty, just as Dante had proposed for the papacy in *Paradiso*. In his sermons he fulminated against the Medici for manipulating politics and religious alliances to extend power in autocratic fashion. He advocated violence

Posthumous portrait of *Lorenzo de' Medici* by Giorgio Vasari, mid-sixteenth century.

(even if only symbolic violence) as a vehicle for deliverance and denounced the Vatican as 'a house of prostitution'. In some way, Savanorola's condemnation of ecclesiastical corruption looked forward to the Protestant Reformation; among his followers were impressionable young men who felt alienated by the money-making of the Medicean Renaissance and who, as a token of their loyalty, gathered up piles of 'heretical' books and paintings and set them ablaze in a giant 'bonfire of the vanities'. These bonfires were symbolic of Savonarola's endeavor to rid Florence of the 'filth of Mammon'. His spiritual ferocity with its taint of nostalgic conservatism recalls that of Dante but, oddly, copies of *The Divine Comedy* were also said to have fetched up on those pyres.

The Ferrara-born Savonarola was courting danger. His own Dominican order was under Medici patronage yet he called down God's wrath on the merchant patrons. His absolutist Christianity with its blood-and-brimstone vision of man's redemption sought to transform Florence into a new Jerusalem where a prelapsarian purity might reign. He commended the state of Adam and Eve before the Fall, just as Dante had done in *The Divine Comedy*, and painted a picture of Hell as a place of vile pain, where bankers and other slaves to cash were wedged in a mass of excrement or some other slime. His verbal polemics steeled the Florentines to run the Medici out of town; and in 1494, after sixty years of iron control, they left the city. When, however, Savonarola sought to challenge the authority of papal Rome, he was excommunicated and, in 1498, burned as a heretic on Piazza della Signoria, soon to be the home of Michelangelo's 'David'. After the immolation his ashes were tipped into the River Arno so that nothing of the firebrand could be salvaged as a relic.

Dante's influence pervades Renaissance Florence. His anti-clerical pronouncements foreshadowed those of Niccolò Machiavelli. Certainly the Renaissance-era political theorist and *testa dura* (hard head) was a great reader of Dante. Like Dante,

Proto-Baroque portrait of Machiavelli by the Tuscan artist Santi di Tito, mid-sixteenth century.

Machiavelli not only exhibited obvious anti-clerical biases, but faced political failure and rejection by the Florentine *patria* he so loved. Many have claimed Dante as a proto-Machiavellian. Was he? Machiavelli may have considered Dante a 'man of genius', but he castigated him for the 'unworthy' attacks made on Florence in *The Divine Comedy*. Machiavelli was not a supporter of Savonarola's Christian-flagellant attempt to morally cleanse Florence (as Dante, had he lived, might have been), yet a Savonarolan part of him surely delighted to see the Medici finally exiled. It was during the post-Medici Republic that Machiavelli made a name for himself as deputy chancellor. Appointed to the position in 1498 he carried out diplomatic missions for the Signoria (city government), much as Dante had done as a prior nearly two centuries earlier, including one to Cesare Borgia, son of Pope Alexander VI. As a diplomat Machiavelli learned much about statecraft and how best to counter an autocratic Medici revival. Just as Dante had likened contemporary Italian politics to life in a brothel, so Machiavelli viewed the papacy as a prime cause of the weakness of Italy and of the decay of religion in Italy. The church was then in its most corrupt phase just before the Reformation; Machiavelli hoped that the corruption might be unravelled to its core but his life was now in danger.

In 1512, following the return of the Medici, Machiavelli was arrested and tortured: the liberty of Florence had come to an end. In prison he continued to study Dante closely, if with a critical eye. Soon into his imprisonment, as if by a miracle, Pope Julius II died and his successor Pope Leo X, Cardinal Giovanni de' Medici, declared a general amnesty for political prisoners. On his release, Machiavelli began to work for the reinstated Medici, writing not only his 1532 political treatise *The Prince* (dedicated to Lorenzo de' Medici), but also a series of books on the nature of republics. Exactly what the Tuscan thinker-diplomat always thought in these acutely intelligent books is not easy to tell because Machiavelli was at times an ironist, whose own views were kept hidden for reasons of political circumspection. His advice either to be like the fox or lion in politics (and thus avoid entrapment) would have baffled Dante, who never played the role of devil's advocate, as Machiavelli, with his bitter jokes and paradoxes, so frequently did. In his unfinished long poem of 1517, 'The Golden Ass', Machiavelli pictures himself as a 'terror-stricken' middle-aged man lost in an alien murky wood. ('I had come to the end of my life, in a dark, cloudy and sunless place.') He is rescued, not by Virgil as in *The Divine Comedy*, but by a Circe-like shepherdess, who comforts him with food and wine before taking him to bed. 'You led me with you, to save me.' Such voluptuary sweetness is quite absent in Dante.

Comparisons with Martin Luther will not really work, either, even though they are often made. The German theologian's campaign to restore biblical Christianity to sixteenth-century Europe helped to ease the way for capitalism and modern secularism, not Luther's intent. But in the Catholic view – essentially, Dante's view – it destroyed the mystery of the sacraments and the magic and pageantry of the Mass. Priceless ecclesiastical treasures were lost in the drive to uproot 'Mass-mongers'. As the Reformation spread across northern Europe, so Dante and his work were twisted into justification for Protestant dissent. Revered as a pioneer of the Reformation, the Florentine was turned into a sort of Italian Lollard.

Of all the books by Dante, none was reckoned to be more anti-papal than *De monarchia* (literally 'Government by One'). Written in exile, it was subjected to a ritual burning in Bologna in 1329 under Pope Giovanni XXII. Dante's own heretical bones might have 'suffered the same fate but for the interference of an influential man of letters, Pino della Tosa', remarked Samuel Beckett. (Della Tosa happened to be in Bologna at the time and was thus able to intervene.) That did not prevent *De monarchia* from being placed on the Index of Forbidden Books in the mid-sixteenth century, where it remained until 1900. The storm of ecclesiastical abuse raised by the book was part of a Counter-Reformation backlash. In Dante's age there was no such thing as a harmless political treatise, or one that was incapable of injuring anybody.

In essence, *De monarchia* argued that the Roman church had corrupted itself by becoming too entangled in secular affairs. From this confusion of powers (Dante believed) derived all contemporary strife and corruption. Like Machiavelli, Dante devoutly wished for a political redeemer to reform the 'Italian' national character, unite the country and establish it as a great European force. For Dante, that saviour was to be Henry VII, count of Luxemburg, who was elected Holy Roman Emperor in 1308, when Dante was six years into his exile and at work on *Purgatorio*. Crowned emperor in 1309, the following year Henry embarked on an expedition to pacify the fractious Italian city-states nominally under his rule, and set the church in order. Dante responded with great enthusiasm to the expedition. The Holy Roman Emperor's divinely ordained authority would, Dante hoped, put an end to the regnant papal claim that it ruled absolutely over the laity. In the final canto of *Purgatorio*, Beatrice prophesizes the imminent arrival of a Messiah-like individual designated by the Roman numeral DXV, believed by many scholars to be a transposition of the Latin *dux* ('leader'). Conceivably this was Henry; by the time Dante came to write *Paradiso*, however, the emperor's expedition had lost what little support it had from the papacy. It ended ignominiously with Henry's early death from malaria in 1313. Dante reserves a seat for him among the blessed in *Paradiso*.

De monarchia was a work of prophetic significance that called for the separation of church and state. In due course such an idea would become central to Enlightenment European political thought and culture; in Dante's time, though, it was inflammatory. The book was circulated at the court of Henry VIII in England at the time of the Protestant Reformation, which is said to have begun on 31 October 1517 when Luther affixed his ninety-five theses to the door of Wittenberg's Castle Church. Within two generations, England's Catholic past was obliterated. Foxe's Book of Martyrs, the most popular religious book in 1560s England, hailed 'Dantes' as a writer who 'declareth the pope to be the whore of Babilon'. For Foxe and other reformers it was easily argued that Dante's Catholicism was evangelical and 'pure' and therefore more like Protestantism than its Roman counterpart. A number of Italians also thought as much. Among them was the Renaissance poet and noblewoman Vittoria Colonna who, unlike her friend and lover, the ambitious cardinal-poet Pietro Bembo, was disturbed by the avariciousness and materialism within the church during the Reformation. She fraternized with such cautious reformers as Cardinal Pole, the future Archbishop of Canterbury, who was resident in Viterbo near Rome in the early 1540s. Like many cultivated Renaissance women, Colonna was attracted to Luther's fiery personality, whose pulpit oratory promised spiritual renewal for Catholic Europe. Although Colonna never abandoned the Church of Rome, she was watched by the guardians of the Inquisition and by the time she died in 1547, a month after Henry VIII, the charges against her as a 'heretic' ran to over three pages. Colonna had written numerous sweet graceful rhymes of love, influenced by Dante and his Florentine successor Petrarch; effectively they are 'revelations of divine love' (to borrow the words of Julian of Norwich).

Henry VIII's first wife, Catherine of Aragon, was another woman said to have admired Dante. Among her possessions was a Castilian translation of the *Inferno* by Pedro Fernández de Villegas, published in Burgos in 1515 (the copy is now in the British Library). The translation reflected Catherine's concern to maintain her Spanish connections and the range of her pious interests. (It was still in Henry VIII's library at Whitehall when an inventory was taken in 1547.) Henry himself had very little interest in religious dogma or doctrine, but his need for divorce from Catherine fuelled his quarrel with the pope. It was only once Anglo-Catholicism had replaced Roman Catholicism that England could save herself and go it alone. The Henrician Reformation was thus driven by more than a king's determination to have a new wife and a male heir. It came to reflect the king's objection to control by a foreign power and his insistence on sovereignty.

By the end of Henry VIII's reign in 1547, twenty-nine editions of *The Divine Comedy* had run off the presses in Italy; imported into England these helped to stoke the cause of the 'King's Reformation'. Above all it was Beatrice's attack in *Paradiso* (canto 29) on the follies and false doctrine of preachers that served to emphasize the contrast between the 'true' church of the gospel and the 'false' church as led by the papal Antichrist:

> Christ did not say to his first holy band,
> 'Go out and preach idle rubbish through the world.'
> He gave them truths and a solid foundation.

The violence and acrimony of Luther's attacks on Catholicism surpassed anything by Dante. Pope Leo X was a 'sodomite' and a 'transvestite', who had subjected the Christian 'family' to levels of 'Satanic' abuse. Marian veneration was scorned as a form of idolatry. In Luther's view, God's Holy Writ had been deformed by Jews and other contaminants within the German heartland. A grievous sense of social inferiority may have motivated these hatreds. Luther had grown up in the provincial mining town of Mansfeld, a hell-pit of smouldering slagheaps and furnaces, where his father was a master smelter. His Jew-baiting, no mere relic of Catholic anti-Semitism, was integral to Protestant identity and a Protestant sense of election as God's anointed people. Only the Bible – *sola scriptura* – could decide matters of liturgy and doctrine. The Bible was superior to the false glitter of popes, councils, church fathers, the Virgin Mary and all those blessed saints. This was emphatically not the language of Dante.

Where Dante had called for the reform of the Catholic church, Luther wished to see its destruction. His doctrinal and liturgical revolution swept all before it, but Dante would have been among the first to repudiate that ambition. As a schismatic, Luther might have kept company with the Prophet Muhammad in the *Inferno*.

It makes more sense to see Luther as 'the Dante of the German language', a comparison which has more than neatness in its favour. Just as Dante had fashioned a literary language from Italy's distinct regional vernaculars, so Luther established a common tongue from the myriad dialects of the Germany of his day, and used this German to translate the Old and New Testaments. Luther's was a heroic undertaking that literally took God's word to the people. Vernacular versions of the Bible provided a useful protest against the licentiousness and unbridled greed of the papacy, with its Boccaccio-like friars and other embarrassments. Luther's translation of the Bible loaded and vivified the German language with coinages that are still in use. Like his contemporary William Tyndale in Reformation England, Luther daringly translated the Greek word *ekklesia* as 'community' or 'congregation' rather than 'church'. Congregational singing – an innovation of the Lutheran revolt – allowed the faithful to become participants in church worship rather than mute spectators. Luther's use of the word 'community' was designed to deprive the church of its resonance as a holy assembly, and undermine the priesthood's sacramental function.

*

Seven hundred years on, Dante remains the hero-saint of vernacular literature in Italy. On its publication in 1978, Primo Levi's novel *The Wrench* (*La chiave a stella*) was seen as a distinguished contribution to the long tradition of Italian regional and dialect literature that began with Dante and the Sicilian poets under King Frederick II. It contained pages of demotically colourful Piedmontese culled from car-repair shops and tinkers' yards on the outskirts of the author's native Turin. Pasolini's dialect-rich novels of the 1950s had been an influence; yet Levi was also familiar with the work of the nineteenth-century Roman dialect poet Giuseppe Gioachino Belli, whose sonnets in Roman vernacular mingled scatology ('dingus', 'todger', 'wanger') with religious themes of death, love and redemption.

In the six years between 1831 and 1837, Belli wrote 2,279 sonnets in *romanesco* (a dialect which even Dante regarded as too coarse for literature). The majority were set amid the card sharps and prostitutes of Rome's Trastevere ('across the Tiber') district, where a monument to the poet stands today. Belli conjured a pre-Risorgimento Rome and the life of its common people with journalistic realism. The sonnets were never intended for publication, as Belli feared charges of obscenity. Instead, he circulated them privately among admirers, among them the Russian writer Nikolai Gogol. Though Belli was a rebel to the point of subversion in his verse, he remained a political and religious conservative, who worked as a censor for the papal government. The grand set pieces of Christian theology were as dear to Belli as they were to Dante. '*Er paradiso*' imagines a heaven where nobody has to work, and where there is a bonus of free food in the shape of the panettone-like '*ppandescèlo*' (which tastes oddly of communion wafer):

in heaven
you don't waste time with any work:
there's nothing but violins, laughter
and heaven's bread

Belli's paradisal 'bread' is a frank allusion the '*pan de li angeli*' (angels' bread) of Dante's imagined Paradise, where there is no room for recreation, sociability or even motion but (as in the Talking Heads song 'Heaven', where 'nothing ever happens') it is blissful to be perfectly still. Anthony Burgess was captivated by Belli's Roman milieu with its Caravaggesque gallery of tavern boys and podgy prelates. His 1977 novel *ABBA ABBA* imagines an encounter in Rome between Belli and the Romantic poet and Dante enthusiast John Keats. Seventy-one of Burgess's own translations of Belli, pitched in what he termed 'English with a Manchester accent', were appended to the novel. These are distinguished by an amusingly vulgar coarseness and the odd flight into Miltonic grandeur.

Shortly before his death in 1863, at the age of seventy-two, Belli asked his friend Monsignor Vincenzo Tizziani (later Bishop of Terni) to burn his Roman poems. Tizziani refused and returned them instead to the poet's son, Ciro Belli, who published them in a four-volume selection in 1865–6. It was from this (severely bowdlerized) edition that one of the first English translations of Belli was made, in 1881, by Frances Eleanor Trollope, sister-in-law of the novelist. It is not known what Trollope made of Belli's more bawdy sonnets, but she was among the earliest English writers to recognize Belli's importance as a sonnet-writer in the *lingua parlata* of Rome. A Dantean influence is everywhere apparent in the sonnets. Belli makes much of rhyming *paradiso* (heaven) with *riso* (smile), just as Dante had done in the third and final canticle of *The Divine Comedy*, where Beatrice is constantly wreathed in smiles.

I first read Dante in Rome where I lived in the 1980s. A secondhand edition of *La divina commedia*, fortified with Gustave Doré's Gothic etchings, had caught my eye. I was in my early twenties. The book, the size of a small encyclopedia, kept me occupied in the autumn of 1984 when, after an unexplained fall, I found myself in a hospital in Rome acutely head-injured and disorientated. (My flatmate had found me sprawled on the floor of our apartment on Via Salaria; the police suspected an intruder, yet nothing was stolen.) On regaining consciousness I saw a group of nuns move past me with elaborate white coifs, each bearing a carafe of white wine. So I was in *Paradiso* – or perhaps a bad

Fellini movie. (The carafes turned out to contain urine samples.) Owing to a shortage of trained nurses, nuns from San Giovanni church nearby acted as paramedics. They suggested that I sleep on the hospital roof during the day as the ward had become so stuffy. It was there, on a terrace overlooking the Egyptian obelisk which Pope Sixtus V had erected in the sixteenth century, that I started to read Dante. Even with my basic Italian I was surprised by how easy *The Divine Comedy* was to read, at least in the sense that T. S. Eliot intended when he said that genuine poetry 'can communicate before it is understood'. I remember that it snowed during my convalescence. It was the first snowfall in Rome for ten years. The city is used to such unseasonal strangeness. Every year in the Roman church of Santa Maria Maggiore a bagful of white petals is shaken free, high up inside the nave, to commemorate the snowfall that occurred in Rome at the height of summer in AD 358. The church, popularly known as Our Lady of the Snow, was most likely visited by Dante in 1300 during Pope Boniface VIII's 'Jubilee Year'. It is situated off Viale Trastevere, where Belli's statue shows a top-hatted man about town.

There is, finally, a family connection with Dante. In 1961, my aunt Maret Haugas was diagnosed with schizophrenia, and sectioned at Hill End psychiatric hospital in St Albans, outside London. In that Victorian-era institution they combined insulin-coma shock therapy with straitjackets and other forms of coercion. At this time my aunt was a student at the Royal College of Art under the supervision of Professor Carel Weight, whose canvases transfigured the streets of London into a suburban apocalypse influenced by Stanley Spencer.

Weight (who is my godfather) identified with my aunt's brittle temperament. Her brooding canvas 'Dark Landscape', painted in about 1959 and now in the British Arts Council Collection, is Weight-like in its haunted strangeness and Dantescan other-worldliness. She pursued the strange logic of her own sensibility in a manner that suggests influences ranging from German Expressionism to Samuel Palmer. Born in 1934 in the medieval Baltic city of Tallinn, my aunt had been forced to flee her home at the end of the war ahead of Stalin's advancing armies. Homesick for a home she no longer had, she became unwell and was eventually unable to distinguish, between the real and the fantastical. She had seen and heard too much; everything in the end demanded too much of her. In 1959, before the illness set in, she went to Italy on a Royal College of Art Travelling Scholarship. Her intention was to research illustrations to Dante, especially those by Botticelli, which she loved. 'I should like to visit Italy', she wrote in her proposal to Professor Weight. 'I have decided to settle down in Florence. I hope to paint in Florence and live there as cheaply as I can.' In *The Divine Comedy* I believe she found an expression of the plight and cultural homelessness of political refugees in post-war Europe; Dante had spoken in *Paradiso* of the 'bitterness' attendant on eating 'strangers' bread' (*lo pane altrui*) and the hardship and humiliation of going up and down another's man's staircase. The first of my aunt's attacks occurred in Florence in the winter of 1960. Paranoid fantasies, bizarre thoughts and hallucinations marked the beginning of a disintegration. For a long time afterwards Carel Weight sent her money and offered to take her out to lunch. ('I was most upset to hear of your illness and how you are suffering. I would like to help you if possible.') The gifted and outwardly undamaged art student he had known before the illness took hold was only waiting to be revealed again, so Weight hoped. My aunt was made a long-term inmate at Hill End, where she continued to paint, chain-smoke cigarettes and read Dante. She died in 2006; none of her Dante illustrations has come to light. My own journey into the life and work of Dante Alighieri must end here.

I have prepared my peace
With learned Italian things

Bibliography

**Books by Dante
in English Translation**

Henry Boyd, *The Divina Commedia of Dante Alighieri: Consisting of the Inferno – Purgatorio – and Paradiso (3 vols),* T. Cadell jun. and W. Davies, London, 1802

Ciaran Carson (trans), *The Inferno of Dante Alighieri,* Granta Books, London, 2002

Henry Francis Cary, *The Vision; or, Hell, Purgatory and Paradise, of Dante Alighieri (3 vols),* Taylor and Hessey, London, 1814

John Ciardi, *The Divine Comedy,* W. W. Norton, New York, 1977

Steve Ellis (trans), *Dante Alighieri: Hell,* Chatto & Windus, London, 1994

Eric Griffiths and Matthew Reynolds (eds), *Dante in English,* Penguin, London, 2005

Samuel Walker Griffith, *The Inferno of Dante Alighieri,* Forgotten Books, London, 2012

A. G. Ferrers Howell (trans), *De vulgari eloquentia,* Rebel Press, London, 1972

Clive James, *Dante: The Divine Comedy,* Picador, London, 2015

Robin Kirkpatrick (trans), *Dante Alighieri: The Divine Comedy,* Penguin, London, 2012

Eugene Lee-Hamilton, *The Inferno of Dante,* Grant Richards, London, 1898

Henry Wadsworth Longfellow, *The Divine Comedy of Dante Alighieri (3 vols),* Ticknor and Fields, Boston, 1867

Anthony Mortimer (trans), *Vita nuova,* Oneworld Classics, London, 2011

J. G. Nichols (trans), *The Divine Comedy,* Alma Classics, Richmond, UK, 2012

J. G. Nichols and Anthony Mortimer (trans), *Rime,* Oneworld Classics, London, 2009

Sean O'Brien (trans), *Dante's Inferno,* Picador, London, 2006

Robert Pinsky (trans), *The Inferno of Dante,* Farrar, Straus and Giroux, New York, 1994

E. H. Plumptre, *The Commedia and Canzoniere of Dante Alighieri,* William Isbister, London, 1886

Christopher Ryan (trans), *The Banquet,* Anma Libri, Saratoga, 1989

Dorothy L. Sayers, *The Comedy of Dante Alighieri: Hell,* Penguin, London, 1949

John Sinclair (trans), *The Divine Comedy of Dante Alighieri,* 3 vols, Oxford University Press, Oxford, 1971

C. H. Sisson (trans), *Dante: The Divine Comedy,* Pan Books, London, 1981

Philip Terry (trans), *Dante's Inferno,* Carcanet, Manchester, 2014

Criticism and Biography

Zygmunt Barański and Lino Pertile (eds), *Dante in Context,* Cambridge University Press, Cambridge, 2015

John C. Barnes and Michelangelo Zaccarello, *Language and Style in Dante,* Four Courts Press, Dublin, 2013

Teodolinda Barolini and H. Wayne Storey (eds), *Dante For the New Millennium,* Fordham University Press, New York, 2003

Teodolinda Barolini, *Dante's Poets: Textuality and Truth in the Comedy,* Princeton University Press, Princeton, 2014

Giovanni Boccaccio, *Life of Dante* (trans Philip Wicksteed), Oneworld Classics, London, 2009

Giovanni Boccaccio, *Boccaccio's Expositions on Dante's Comedy* (trans and ed Michael Papo), University of Toronto Press, Toronto, 2009

Michael Caesar (ed), *Dante: The Critical Heritage,* Routledge, London, 1989

Stefano Carrai, *La lirica Toscana del Duecento: cortesi, guittoniani, stilnovisti,* Laterza, Rome, 1997

Isabelle Chabot, 'Il Matrimonio di Dante', in *Reti Medievali Rivista,* 15, 2 (2014)

Elizabeth A. Coggeshall, 'Dante, Islam, and Edward Said', in *Telos,* Summer 2007

T. S. Eliot, *Selected Essays,* Faber, London, 1961

Steve Ellis, *Dante and English Poetry,* Cambridge University Press, Cambridge, 1983

Joan M. Ferrante, *The Political Vision of the Divine Comedy,* Princeton University Press, Princeton, 1984

John Freccero, *Dante: The Poetics of Conversion,* Harvard University Press, Harvard, 1986

Simon A. Gilson, *Dante and Renaissance Florence,* Cambridge University Press, Cambridge, 2005

Guglielmo Gorni, *Giudo Cavalcanti: Dante e il suo 'primo amico',* Aracne, Rome, 2009

Antonio Gramsci, *Prison Notebooks* (ed and trans Joseph A. Buttigieg and Antonio Callari), Vol 2, Notebook 4, Columbia University Press, New York, 2011

Cecil Grayson (ed), *The World of Dante: Essays on Dante and his Times,* Clarendon Press, Oxford, 1980

Cecil Grayson, 'Latin and Vernacular in Dante's Thought', in *Centenary Essays on Dante,* Clarendon Press, Oxford, 1965

Peter Hainsworth and David Robey, *Dante: A Very Short Introduction,* Oxford University Press, Oxford, 2015

Robert Hollander, *Studies in Dante,* Longo Editore, Ravenna, 1980

Rachel Jacoff, *The Cambridge Companion to Dante,* Cambridge University Press, Cambridge, 1993

Tristan Kay, Martin McLaughlin, Michelangelo Zaccarello (eds), *Dante in Oxford: The Paget Toynbee Lectures,* Routledge, London, 2006

Tristan Kay, *Dante's Lyric Redemption: Eros, Salvation, Vernacular Tradition,* Oxford University Press, Oxford, 2016

Dennis Looney, *Freedom Readers: The African American Reception of Dante Alighieri and the Divine Comedy,* University of Notre Dame Press, Indiana, 2011

Vittorio Montemaggi, *Reading Dante's Commedia as Theology,* Oxford University Press, Oxford, 2016

Miguel Asin Palacios, *Islam and the Divine Comedy,* Goodword Books, Delhi, 2001

Emanuela Patti, *Pasolini after Dante: The 'Divine Mimesis' and the Politics of Representation,* Routledge, London, 2016

Barbara Reynolds, *Dante: The Poet, the Political Thinker, the Man,* I. B. Tauris, 2006

Barbara Reynolds, *The Passionate Intellect: Dorothy L. Sayers' Encounter with Dante,* Wipf and Stock, Oregon, 2005

Marco Santagata, *Dante: The Story of His Life,* Belknap Press, London, 2016

John A. Scott, *Understanding Dante,* University of Notre Dame Press, Notre Dame, Indiana, 2004

Prue Shaw, *Reading Dante: From Here to Eternity*, Liverlight Publishing Corporation, New York, 2104

John Addington Symonds, *An Introduction to Dante*, Adam & Charles Black, London, 1899

John Took, *Dante: Lyric Poet and Philosopher: An Introduction to the Minor Works*, Clarendon Press, Oxford, 1990

Charles Williams, *The Figure of Beatrice: A Study in Dante*, Faber & Faber, London, 1943

Ernesto Zingarelli, 'Parole e forme della *Divina Commedia* aliene dal dialetto fiorentino', in *Studi di Filogolgia Romanza*, Ermano Loescher & Co, Rome, 1888

Dante's World

Harold Acton and Edward Chaney (eds), *Florence: A Traveller's Companion*, Constable, London, 1986

Hunt Emerson and Kevin Jackson, *Dante's Inferno*, Knockabout Ltd, London, 2012

James Fenton, 'Il miglior fabbro: on English translations of Dante', in *Guardian*, 25 June 2005

John Freccero, *In Dante's Wake: Reading from Medieval to Modern in the Augustinian Tradition*, Fordham University Press, New York, 2016

Eric G. Haywood (ed), *Dante Metamorphosis: Episodes in a Literary Life*, Four Courts Press, Dublin, 2003

Francesca Klein (ed), *Il libro del chiodo*, Edizioni Polistampa, Florence, 2004

Dagmar Korbacher, *Botticelli and Treasures from the Hamilton Collection*, The Courtauld Gallery, London, 2106

Joseph Luzzi, *In a Dark Wood: What Dante Taught Me About Grief, Healing, and the Mysteries of Love*, Collins, London, 2015

Anthony Mortimer (trans), *Complete Poems: Guido Cavalcanti*, Alma Classics, London, 2010

Tim Parks, 'A Most Delicate Invention: Money and Beauty', in *London Review of Books*, 22 September 2011

Tim Parks, 'Guelfs v. Ghibellines', in *London Review of Books*, 14 July 2016

Matthew Pearl, *The Dante Club*, Vintage, London, 2004

Ralph Pite, *The Circle of Our Vision: Dante's Presence in English Romantic Poetry*, Oxford University Press, Oxford, 1994

Dante Gabriel Rossetti, *The Early Italian Poets from Ciullo d'Alcamo to Dante Alighieri (1100-1200-1300)*, Smith, Elder & Co, London, 1861

Other Sources, Essays and Papers

Baraka Amiri, *The System of Dante's Hell*, Akashic Books, New York, 2016

Tim Ashley, 'Hell on Earth', in *Guardian*, 8 January 2005

Samuel Beckett, *Poems in English*, John Calder, London, 1961

Samuel Beckett, *Echo's Bones*, Faber, London, 2014

Samuel Beckett, *How It Is*, John Calder, London, 1964

Samuel Beckett, *More Pricks Than Kicks*, Calder and Boyars, London, 1970

Samuel Beckett, *Molloy*, Calder and Boyars, London, 1971

Samuel Beckett, *Texts for Nothing*, Calder and Boyars, 1974

Samuel Beckett, *The Letters of Samuel Beckett 1957–1965*, Cambridge University Press, Cambridge, 2014

Samuel Beckett, 'Dante...Bruno. Vico...Joyce', in *Our Exagmination Round His Factification for Incamination of Work in Progress*, Faber and Faber, London, 1958

Erica Benner, *Be Like the Fox: Machiavelli's Lifelong Quest for Freedom*, Allen Lane, London, 2017

David Bindman, Stephen Hebron, Michael O'Neill, *Dante Rediscovered: From Blake to Rodin*, The Wordsworth Trust, Grasmere, 2007

William Blake, *The Divine Comedy*, Bibliotèque de l'Image, Paris, 2000

Jorge Luis Borges, *Seven Nights*, Faber, London, 1984

Lucrezia Borgia and Pietro Bembo, *The Prettiest Love Letters in the World,* Collins, London, 1988

George Bornstein, 'Yeats's Romantic Dante', in *Colby Quarterly,* Maine, vol. 15, June 1979

Dan Brown, *Inferno,* Bantam, London, 2013

William Burroughs, *The Naked Lunch,* John Calder/Olympia Press, London, 1966

William Burroughs, *Cities of the Red Night,* John Calder, London, 1981

Italo Calvino (ed Martin McLaughlin), *Letters: 1941–1985,* Princeton University Press, Princeton, 2013

Enrico Cerulli, *Il Libro della Scala e la questione delle fonti arabo-spagnole della Divina Commedia,* Biblioteca Apostolica Vaticana, Rome, 1949

Jessie Childs, *God's Traitors: Terror and Faith in Elizabethan England,* Bodley Head, London, 2014

Robert Crawford, *Young Eliot: From St Louis to The Waste Land,* Jonathan Cape, 2015

Vincent Cronin, *The Florentine Renaissance,* Pimlico, London, 1992

Andrea Del Cornò, 'Letture e libri italiani nella Londra vittoriana: la bottega libraria dei fratelli Rolandi di Quarona', in 'Le fusa del gatto', Società Bibliografica Toscana, Torrita di Siena, 2015

Andrea Del Cornò, 'Un ritrovato giornale mazziniano: "Il Pellegrino"', in 'Le fusa del gatto', Società Bibliografica Toscana, Torrita di Siena, 2013

Paolo De Ventura, 'Dante e Maometto: ragguagli ultimi di una lunga polémcia', in *Critica Letteraria* N. 168–9, 2015

Eamon Duffy, *Reformation Divided: Catholics, Protestants and the Conversion of England,* Bloomsbury, London, 2017

Jeremy Dummett, *Palermo: City of Kings,* I. B. Tauris, London, 2015

T. S. Eliot, *The Poems of T. S. Eliot,* Vol 1, Faber and Faber, London, 2015

Richard Ellmann, *James Joyce,* Oxford University Press, Oxford, 1982

M. Salem Elsheikh, 'Lettura (faziosa) dell'episodio di Muhammad', in *Quaderni di filologia romanza,* Vol 23, no. 2, 2015

Evelyn Fishburn and Psiche Hughes, *A Dictionary of Borges,* Duckworth, London, 1990

John Flaxman, *Compositions by John Flaxman, Sculptor, R.A., from the Divine Poem of Dante Alighieri, Containing Hell, Purgatory and Paradise, With Quotations from the Italian, and Translations from the Version of the Reverend H. Boyd, to Each Plate,* Longman, Hurst, Rees, and Orme, London, 1807

Henry Fuseli, *Henry Fuseli 1741–1825,* Tate Gallery, London, 1975

Edward Hirsch, 'A Fresh Hell', in the *New Yorker,* 23 January 1995

Richard Holmes, *Coleridge: Darker Reflections,* HarperCollins, London, 1998

Amilcare A. Iannucci, *Dante, Cinema and Television,* University of Toronto Press, Toronto, 2004

Gabriel Josipovici, *The World and the Book,* Macmillan, London, 1971

James Knowlson, *The Life of Samuel Beckett,* Bloomsbury, London, 1996

Ed Krčma, *Rauschenberg/Dante,* Yale University Press, London, 2017

Ed Krčma, 'Dating the Dante drawings: Rauschenberg and method', in the *Burlington Magazine,* December 2017

Oscar Kuhns, 'Dante's Influence on Shelley', in *Modern Language Notes,* Vol 13, No 6, June 1898

Robert Lowell, *The Letters of Robert Lowell,* Faber & Faber, London, 2005

Malcolm Lowry, *Sursum Corda! The Collected Letters of Malcolm Lowry, Vol 1: 1926–46,* Jonathan Cape, London, 1995

Lauro Martines, *April Blood: Florence and the Plot against the Medici,* Jonathan Cape, London, 2003

Jamie McKendrick, 'Beyond the Human', *London Review of Books,* 26 March 2009

Mario Nagari, *Pietro Rolandi da Quarona a Valesia: 1801–1863,* La Moderna Novara, 1959

Pier Paolo Pasolini, *La Divina Mimesis*, Einaudi, Turin, 1975

Walter Pater, *The Renaissance*, Macmillan, London, 1910

Jan Piggott, *Palace of the People: The Crystal Palace at Sydenham 1854–1936*, C. Hurst & Co, London, 2004

Donato Pirovano, 'I controversi rapporti tra Dante e la letteratura islamica', in *L'Indice*, March 2014

Ezra Pound, *The Cantos of Ezra Pound*, Faber & Faber, London, 1987

Craig Raine, *The Divine Comedy*, Atlantic Books, London, 2012

Matthew Reynolds, 'Jamming up the Flax Machine', in the *London Review of Books*, 8 May 2003

Lucy Riall, *Garibaldi: Invention of a Hero*, Yale University Press, London, 2004

Nicholas Roe, *John Keats: A New Life*, Yale University Press, London, 2012

Anthony Rudolf, 'Memory and Writing', in *Stand 5* (3) 2004

Gaia Servadio, *Renaissance Women*, I.B.Tauris, London, 2005

Prue Shaw, 'The Fires of Lust and Poetry', in *Lectura Dantis* (ed Allen Mandelbaum, Anthony Oldcorn, Charles Ross), University of California Press, 2008

Enzo Siciliano, *Pasolini*, Bloomsbury, London, 1987

Denis Mack Smith, *Mazzini*, Yale University Press, London, 1994

Mike Stocks (trans) *Sonnets: Giuseppe Gioacchino Belli*, Oneworld Classics, London, 2007

Paul Strathern, *Death in Florence: The Medici, Savonarola and the Battle for the Soul of the Renaissance City*, Jonathan Cape, London, 2011

Paul Strathern, *The Medici: Godfathers of the Renaissance*, Jonathan Cape, London, 2003

Ian Thomson, *Primo Levi: Una Vita*, UTET, Milan, 2017

Ian Thomson, 'Roman Todger', article on Giuseppe Gioacchino Belli, *Times Literary Supplement*, 30 January 2009

Ian Thomson, 'The trump and the rump', review of Ciaran Carson's *The Inferno of Dante Alighieri*, Guardian, 21 December 2002

Ian Thomson, 'A Divine Journey to Hell and Back', article on Dante, *Independent*, 23 May 2015

Ian Thomson, 'Pretty Pickle', review of J. G. Nichols's translation of *The Divine Comedy*, Times Literary Supplement, 28 June 2013

Ian Thomson, 'Zozzo mondo', article on Pier Paolo Pasolini, *Times Literary Supplement*, 21 November 2008

Ian Thomson, 'Cold War Dante', review of Ed Krčma's *Rauschenberg/Dante*, Times Literary Supplement, 15 September 2017

Ian Thomson, 'Outrageous', review of J. G. Nichols' translation of Boccaccio's *The Decameron*, Times Literary Supplement, 10 September 2010

Ian Thomson, 'In Calvino Veritas', article on Italo Calvino, *Independent on Sunday*, 16 February 1992

James Thomson, *The City of Dreadful Night and Other Poems*, P. J. and A. E. Dobell, London, 1922

Paget Toynbee, 'Diminutive Editions of the *Divina Commedia*', letter in *The Times*, 5 February 1912

Helen Vendler, 'Dante's Vita Nova', in *New Republic*, 5 October 2012

Bill W and Dr Bob, *Alcoholics Anonymous Big Book*, Alcoholics Anonymous World Services Inc., New York, 2001

Garry Wills, *Why I am a Catholic*, Houghton Mifflin Company, New York, 2002

W. B. Yeats, 'William Blake and his illustrations to the *Divine Comedy*', in the *Savoy*, No 3, July 1896

Jan M. Ziolkowsi, 'Dante and Islam', in *Dante Studies*, No 125, 2007

Acknowledgements

Among the living and the dead, special thanks are due to
Dr Ambrogio Camozzi Pistoja at Pembroke College,
Cambridge, who did me the honour of reading chapters in
progress, and whose knowledge of Dante I hold in very high
regard. I am also especially grateful to Dr Paolo De Ventura at
the University of Birmingham, who likewise made me the gift
of his support and suggestions. Freya Dean and Andrew Kenrick
have all my appreciation for their illuminating criticism. I thank
too my dear friend Gaia Servadio for her valuable leads in
researching this little book, and who introduced me to Franco
Zeffirelli's adopted son, Filippo. I would also like to thank Mark
Thompson for once again taking out time from his own writing
to look at the work-in-progress. His encouragement, advice, and
loyalty are priceless.

I am indebted to Neil Belton for commissioning this book;
I trust his judgment absolutely and am grateful for his impeccable
ear for language. Thanks also to Georgina Blackwell and Christian
Duck at Head of Zeus, and to Susan Opie for copy-editing.

In addition I would like to express my warm thanks to
Andrea Del Cornò, Italian Acquisitions Officer at the London
Library, for his help in writing about the 'Altissimo Poeta' (as
Antonio Panizzi called Dante); with Andrea's generosity and help
in tracking down articles on the world of Dante I was better able
to finish the project on time. My thanks are further due to Dr Jan
Piggott, who gave me my first introduction to the world of letters,
and to his wife Cas. They accompanied me along the sometimes
thorny way of writing about *The Divine Comedy*. Dr Catherine

Keen at University College London kindly made her Dante bibliography available to me, while Ed Krçma at the University of East Anglia helped me more than he might have suspected (thank you for putting me in the way of curious Dante-related books and for reading that chapter). I also owe grateful thanks to my colleagues at UEA, comrades in arms in the sometimes awkward world of campus politics: Helen Smith and Kathryn Hughes. My friend Saskia Baron first alerted me to Rauschenberg's visualizations of Dante. Thank you for that.

I thank, too, the following people for their assistance and encouraging persistence: Sean Robinson, friend and tip top sponsor, who has helped to sustain me in the dry season and introduced me to *L'Inferno* the movie, Lily Pizzichini, Will Rossiter, medievalist extraordinaire, Ciaran Carson, Miguel ('Migz') Cullen, Robert Gordon, Stephen Massil, Cecilia Robustelli, Tony Rudolf, Filippo ('Pippo') Zeffirelli, Weston Charlesworth, Rebecca Stott, Marco Delogu at the Italian Cultural Institute (London), and Neil Parkinson, Archives and Collections Manager at the Royal College of Art. Dr Emanuela Patti at the University of Birmingham led me towards a greater understanding of Pasolini's indebtedness to Dante. I am deeply grateful to the spirit of my aunt, Maret, who I sometimes believe was present. Thanks are due also to Father Terry Tastard and Father Leo Edgar, who know so much about the mysteries at the heart of life, and to Maurice Glasman, for the fifteen years of our friendship. May Jah be with you.

Laura (unknown to me, a potential Beatrice) helpfully commented on the early chapters in draft: here's to the imperishable memory of old times. Maud, Sidney and Henry have been tolerant of the many hours over the many years when I retreated into my own little world in order to write or simply to avoid doing the washing up. (Henry: a special thanks to you for the Doom leads, which were cool and good.) I love you all.

Index